The Changing American Newspaper

THE CHANGING
AMERICAN NEWSPAPER

HERBERT BRUCKER

ASSISTANT TO THE DEAN
GRADUATE SCHOOL OF JOURNALISM
COLUMBIA UNIVERSITY

NEW YORK

COLUMBIA UNIVERSITY PRESS

1937

To S. S. C.

At Deadline

WHEN HARRY L. GAGE, vice-president of the Mergenthaler Linotype Company, was talking shop in a newspaper office the other day he spoke of some experimental work at the Graduate School of Journalism in Columbia University. He remarked that one of the experiments dealt with an odd-sized newspaper page containing five wide columns in large type instead of the usual eight narrow ones in small type, and that the resulting page size, if adopted, would make every newspaper press in the country obsolete. A newspaper press to print such a page, in other words, does not exist.

"Isn't that just like a bunch of college professors," said one of the newspaper men.

It is. One of a university's functions is to investigate those fields which men on the job find impractical. It has happened that such investigations have ultimately found practical use.

This book has been written in the hope that, to some extent, it may be useful in this way. The American newspaper is changing once more. Various aspects of these changes are analyzed in the pages which follow, and some of the further forms which may result are discussed. Throughout attention has been centered on adapting the newspaper to the needs of the reader under modern social conditions.

Acknowledgments are due to The Atlantic Monthly for permis-

sion to reprint Chapter I, and to The Independent Journal of
Columbia University for permission to reprint Chapters II to VII,
all in revised form. Primarily, however, my indebtedness is to Dean
Carl W. Ackerman of the Graduate School of Journalism, without
whose support this book would not exist. Grateful thanks are likewise due to Douglas Southall Freeman, editor of The Richmond
News Leader, and to George H. Gallup, director of the American
Institute of Public Opinion, both of whom are pioneers on the
frontiers of journalism, and to others of the faculty of the Graduate School of Journalism for advice and inspiration. Ideas and en-
couragement have been drawn from many editors, notably J. Roscoe Drummond and Volney D. Hurd of The Christian Science
Monitor, George Fort Milton and J. Charles Poe of The Chattanooga News, Arthur Sinnott of The Newark Evening News, Lowell
Mellett of The Washington News, Leon S. Dure, Jr., of The Richmond Times-Dispatch, Wilbur Forrest and Grafton Wilcox of The
New York Herald Tribune, and Robert E. Garst and Theodore
Menline Bernstein of The New York Times. Finally, through the
friendly help of Harry L. Gage and John E. Allen of the Mergenthaler Linotype Company some of the theories advanced in this
book have been given the critical test of type.

To these and other men, and to still others known to me by their
work rather than by name, I wish to express my gratitude. All of
them must be absolved from responsibility for what is said, for the
opinions expressed are my own.

H. B.

Garden City, N.Y.
July 2, 1937

Contents

Present-day headlines are confined within limits too narrow to permit them to function adequately. They are becoming simpler, but might become still more simple. There is also need for less contrast between the largest and smallest heads in the schedule.

No editor would break up his finance or sports department and print one story from it on each page throughout the paper. Conversely, if all stories were grouped into categories of related matter the reader could grasp the whole more readily.

By and large the experience of the three most completely departmentalized newspapers—The Palm Beach Times, The Daytona Beach Morning Journal, and The Richmond Times-Dispatch —has been favorable.

The inverted-pyramid form of news story leads to irritating repetition and confusion. Changing the structure of the story so that each item of news is told adequately, but once only, would avoid repetition, allow more dramatic treatment, and encourage condensation of the news.

A phrase from Kantian metaphysics aptly describes a central factor in newswriting, namely, the necessity of putting the reader into direct contact with the event of which he reads. This leads to more interesting copy. It also makes for more courageous and accurate reporting.

———

Some examples of the Changing American Newspaper.

The Glut of Occurrences

EVEN IN THE COMPLEX SOCIETY of today the function of the press differs little from what it was when the first American newspaper, Publick Occurrences, appeared on Sept. 25, 1690. Benjamin Harris, the publisher, said in his first and only issue: "It is designed, that the Countrey shall be furnished once a moneth (or if any Glut of Occurrences happen, oftener,) with an account of such considerable things as have arrived unto our Notice." Harris promised a faithful relation of memorable occurrents of Divine Providence in order "that people everywhere may better understand the Circumstances of Publique Affairs, both abroad and at home." He also wanted to do something toward "the Curing, or at least the Charming of that Spirit of Lying, which prevails amongst us," and which inevitably prevails where there is no newspaper.

Harris, in short, promised an accurate account of what was happening in the world—that is to say, news. So it has been in American journalism ever since, with variations in treatment and technique necessitated by changes in the social scene. Once the essential sameness of the newspaper's task in any society has been granted, however, it is necessary to note that from time to time changes in the manner of performing that task become necessary.

In other words a newspaper, anywhere, at any time, is substantially the same thing. News is not.

I

The Saturday news-review department "It Happened This Week" was introduced by The New York Sun on December 26, 1931. This is the first of many signposts of recent years which point toward the newspaper of tomorrow. Since then many others have appeared. For four years The Richmond News Leader in Virginia has abandoned its entire Saturday editorial page to an interpretive summary of the week's news. Every week the Associated Press feature department distributes by mail a one-page week-end review of the news, a service which may be supplemented by late wire reviews if desired.

The New York Times began in January, 1935, to give two full pages each Sunday to an illustrated noninterpretive summary of the week's happenings. The Washington Post had the same idea independently, but began publishing a few weeks later, putting slightly more interpretation into its review than does the Times. Numerous others have followed in this path, as for example The New York World-Telegram and The Chicago Tribune. And early in 1937 The Buffalo Times began a daily rather than a weekly news-review on the front page of its second section.

For the most part, however, these ventures remain week-end adjuncts to the daily newspapers rather than models for it. At the same time there have been creeping into the dailies here and there experiments in news writing or news presentation, which indicate that editors are becoming dissatisfied with orthodox newspaper technique. Simpler, cleaner headlines have been introduced by The Cleveland News, again an example followed elsewhere, notably by The Los Angeles Times. Even briefer, more dynamic headlines have been tried by The Chattanooga News, and on March 1, 1937, a radical change in typography was introduced by The Glendale News-Press in California. Last May, too, The New York Journal introduced a front page on which the name plate or masthead was shifted from its traditional position at the top to the left top, allowing room for a dramatic picture display alongside at the top right. This is almost identical with a front-page layout prepared at the Graduate School of Journalism at Columbia in 1934. All in all sweeping changes in typography, plus a rapid evolution of news pictures toward the unposed rather than the formal picture, are the most noticeable if not the most profound signs that the American press is striving for something more adapted to the modern order.

Meanwhile more concise, nonrepetitious news writing appears in the Boston Today section of The Christian Science Monitor. Stories continued from page one have been abolished by several papers, among them The Wisconsin State Journal, which is making other interesting typographic and editorial experiments.

The Washington Star pioneered in November, 1935, with background paragraphs of explanatory material displayed between headline and text of important news stories. Here again is an example being followed elsewhere. The Boise Capital News has made what is perhaps the most radically visible change of all. Instead of the usual selection of important news stories, the front page contains a guide to all important stories throughout the paper. Finally, at the beginning of October, 1936, The Palm Beach Times and The Daytona Beach News-Journal began, each independently and in different fashion, to classify all the news, from page one to the end. Of the Palm Beach experiment the late Marlen Pew said in Editor & Publisher: "It is the most orderly daily newspaper I have ever seen, and I would like to read it daily. I miss my guess if this form is not adopted by scores of newspapers within months."

In a sense this comment was prophetic, for on March 30, 1937, The Richmond Times-Dispatch in Virginia became the first larger paper to departmentalize its columns entirely. And on June 28 The New York Times, advertising the promotion of its news-index from the back page to the first page of its second section, said:

The New York Times is . . . so well arranged that the reader can quickly and easily find the news and departments of particular interest.

The News Index, now appearing on the first page of the second section, tells on what pages certain departments of news appear—financial, sports, obituaries, society, the theater, and many others.

Also important is the effort to which the Times goes to provide
an orderly arrangement of the news for the reader. News stories on
the major topics of the day are grouped on consecutive pages.
Classification in make-up is a great convenience to the reader.

The Times, always a carefully made-up paper according to orthodox standards, is still a long way from complete classification or departmentalization of all its news. Nevertheless its statement is one
more indication of the recognition by newspapers of the need for
greater organization of the news on behalf of the reader.

Meanwhile one continues to hear from laymen enthusiastic if not
always well-informed criticism of the newspaper as it is. The complaints of scientists, educators, and all sorts of observers of public
affairs are well known. More significant, perhaps, is the soul-search-
ing among editors and publishers themselves. At the 1934 meeting
of the American Society of Newspaper Editors, J. Charles Poe of
The Chattanooga News said:

Pick up the average newspaper and what do you read? We still find,
in great abundance, items dealing with petty police court gossip, crimes
of little or no moment, divorce cases, the doings of a movie star,
town or county council meetings, ambulance runs, a Y.M.C.A. membership drive, a school commencement exercise, resolutions by women's
clubs denouncing war in time of peace and urging patriotism in time
of war; the misadventures of a Senator, or the daily doings of an air
hero, the debates over tariff or soldier bonus and a thousand and one
other items no different from those of a hundred years ago. It is the
mere surface of the stream of life and it is no wonder that Professor
Gallup's surveys reveal a distressingly low reader interest in such
so-called news. . . .

Our own experience, after starting a page, one day a week, devoted
to modern trends in education and science, shows by the fine reader
response that the public is willing to read about the new movements in
social fields treated as news and not as sensation or as stunts.

This and other efforts of our paper cause me to suspect that the
press has been guilty of talking down to its readers. We have assumed that their intelligence averaged about that of a third-grader
and printed a paper accordingly. Some say that the press moulds
and leads public opinion, others that it but mirrors the life of its
time. Sometimes I fear that in our news columns we do neither, but

that we lag far behind in supplying that which the public is really capable of understanding and which, in its inarticulate way, it sincerely wants to get.

Or, again, as Stanley Walker put it,

Few students of the trends in news coverage of recent years have given credit to the changes, sometimes almost imperceptible to the general reader, which may be laid to the influence of the news magazine Time and to the New Yorker. These weeklies, although different in appeal, nevertheless have demonstrated what some people suspected all along—that facts, marshaled in smart, orderly fashion, can be charming. . . . The New Yorker . . . has made money by treating its readers, not as pathological cases or a congregation of oafs, but as fairly intelligent persons who want information and entertainment.

At this point anyone who watched the citizenry eating alive the verbatim testimony of the Hauptmann trial while the President's message on social security in the same paper went unread may pause, disillusioned. And yet, one is haunted by the possibilities: "The mere surface of the stream of life" versus "facts, marshaled in smart, orderly fashion." Suppose some publisher took his courage along while he went digging beneath the surface of the news. Suppose we found a way to abolish the headline heterogeneity of the American newspaper and printed instead a smooth, ordered, and well buttressed story of the world each day. With what refreshment of spirit our congregation of oafs would beat a path to the news stands!

Small wonder, then, that since the war there has been recurring gossip to the effect that so-and-so was going to bring out a new newspaper, new not in being merely another added to the existing ones, but new in what it is and does. At least one such project reached the stage of staff organization, though nothing ever came of it. And now it would surprise no newspaperman, I think, if any day there were to appear a newspaper bringing a wholly fresh approach to the age-old task of journalism.

II

In former days the method of presenting separate stories on the day's happenings as they came along was entirely adequate, as indeed it still is with many an item today. Yet as the increasing complexity of the world becomes more apparent, as the reader finds that his own interests reach more and more out of the familiar circle of his daily life into the unknown fields of economics and the other social sciences, this method often leads to bewilderment.

Newspaper editors have recognized this, especially in the years since the war. They often summarize all the stories devoted to some big news event in front-page boxes. For otherwise, in the endeavor to give all the news, these stories are spread over so many columns, or even pages, that the reader, appalled, is likely to turn to his radio news commentator for relief. On page one of The New York Times on the morning these lines are written, for example, appears the news that the Spanish rebels have taken the key defenses of Madrid. This was considered by the editors the most important article of several which dealt with the revolution. But because these related articles were displayed on three different pages of the paper, there was printed immediately under the page-one headline of the rebel success a group of five bulletins summarizing as many stories on the Spanish civil war and its repercussions in Europe. Even so, two major news items on the same subject, and several minor ones, receive no mention in the front-page summaries.

A different use of the same principle may be seen in the Times's customary Sunday front-page bulletin, set two columns wide and headed, "Results in Major Sports Yesterday." This summary tells under four subheads the news of tennis, rowing, baseball, and racing. Without it the reader would have to absorb the message of nine headlines over six columns of stories on four different pages before getting the same news. Even all this is inadequate, again, because about four pages of other sport news are not included in the front-page bulletin.

There is, however, more to this matter of smooth, ordered news presentation than mere summaries, mere boiling down. For just as there are signs that editors are feeling their way toward something new, so there are signs that readers want something new. They want, I think, far more than they now get of those twin imponderables familiar to newspaper men as background and interpretation.

How else can one account for the success of Time magazine, of the radio news commentators, of current-events lecturers, indeed for the rise of interpretive writers in the newspapers themselves? A news-hungry public apparently does not find what it seeks in its own news columns. As one woman's-club member recently told another on leaving a current-events lecture—and this tale is not apocryphal—"Well, now I won't have to read the papers for two weeks."

In its simplest form this factor missing from the news is something which the reporter tends to omit from his account because he knows all about it, whereas the reader does not. The point is made clear in a review of D. W. Brogan's Government of the People, which says:

> The interest in Dr. Brogan's work is heightened by the fact that, writing as an Englishman for Englishmen about our outlandish political institutions, he has occasion to explain many simple features which our own people do not understand but which our own authors would be ashamed to explain in an adult work.

Every day American reporters seem equally reluctant to include obvious but necessary facts in their stories. For example, an Associated Press dispatch before me, one of a collection made as the ideas here presented were growing, appeared in The New York Herald Tribune under the head "Pickets Awed, Permit Kohler To Enter Plant." The story begins:

> KOHLER, WIS., July 17.—The ill blast of strike winds swept today through this "ideal village," dedicated to an idyllic industrialism.
> The situation was epitomized in the lonely stalking through lines of pickets to the administration of the Kohler Company of Walter J. Kohler, former Governor of this state and builder of the model places and village. He lives here and has been an intimate of many of the residents.

For seven more paragraphs the story runs on. It tells the details of Mr. Kohler's lone parade through the picket lines to his office, and gives other bits of spot news. It even tells some facts about this unique industrial village, where labor troubles have been unknown for the twenty years of its existence. It tells everything, indeed, except the news, namely: How and why did a strike come about in this strikeless community?

Presumably no reader of that morning's New York newspapers yet knows. And not a day goes by but that many stories like this are offered to American readers on the theory that they contain all the news that's fit to print, rather than the mere surface of the stream of life. That is what I mean by saying that the reader often misses entirely the element of essential background in the news stories which he may read.

It also happens, however, that laymen miss interpretation in the news columns. And this, of course, is deliberately left out on suspicion that it harbors that antichrist of the newspaper man—opinion. Perhaps, therefore, it will help clear the way if we admit these two things:

1. That it is the function of the reporter to tell what happened, and not what he thinks about what happened.

2. That even where opinion is allowed, as on the editorial page, fact is often more desirable than opinion. Thus it is better to scrap an editorial calling the mayor a liar and a crook, and to write another which, by reciting facts without using adjectives and without calling names, makes it obvious that the mayor is a liar and a crook.

Having granted this, one must grant further that to write interpretation into the news may at times mean straying from pure fact into opinion. Yet this, I submit, is not so fearsome as it sounds. American journalism is conducted upon the assumption that news is fact and editorials are opinion, and never the twain shall meet. That this is infinitely superior to the Continental method of coloring the news to suit one's fancy is not open to question. At the same time the absolute validity of the American doctrine is doubtful. The line between news and opinion is sometimes hard to draw. "The speech was enthusiastically received," records one reporter, while the man next him at the press table writes that it "received a fair scattering of applause." Again, the headlines on page one of the Times and Herald Tribune on stories dealing with the identical event began on October 23, 1934, as follows:

Times:

BANKING LEADERS
BACK COOPERATION
WITH WASHINGTON

Herald Tribune:

BANKERS FIRE
ON NEW DEAL
DESPITE TRUCE

Which was fact, and which opinion?

Possibly American newspaper readers unconsciously realize the difficulty of separating fact from opinion. Perhaps they are willing, the gospel of American journalism to the contrary, to swallow them both together. Indeed, I believe that they are ready to have a certain type of editorial written into their news, without typographical differentiation or any other attempt to set one off from the other.

If any newspaper man is hardy enough to read beyond that statement, he will recall that most editorials fit into one of two classes —the explanatory and the argumentative. Explanatory editorials undertake simply to clarify some event, the news reports of which have left the reader uncertain or bewildered. Argumentative editorials, by contrast, seek to induce the reader to be for or against something. Obviously, it is only the explanatory editorials which might be lifted from our editorial pages and written into the news. Surely this is not so radical as it sounds. It has been done since the year one in American journalism, by political reporters, foreign correspondents, Washington men, and a few other privileged creatures. Why confine it to them?

The thing may become clearer by citing an example. One of the many big news stories of post-war years which are noteworthy for the point under discussion is England's going off the gold standard on September 21, 1931. Now this was news according to both the man-bites-dog school, which considers the unusual or spectacular as news, and a newer school which finds reader interest in the significance and meaning of an event. This newer school, of course, calls into question the classic dogma of newspaper men that the public will not read news merely because it is important. Certainly anyone who has written on current events has been appalled by the apathy with which the public greets the pearls he casts before them. Yet individual members of that same public, when they meet him, say, "Oh, you must know about this Spanish (or old age pension, or C.I.O.) business. Please tell me what it all means." Perhaps, then, it is not the important news that is dull so much as the manner in which it is presented to the news-hungry reader.

So it was at the time of England's departure from the gold standard. For example, The New York Times, always anxious to print all the news, gave this event fifteen stories covering more than thirteen columns on the day the news broke. But nowhere could the persistent reader, even though he staggered on down to the bottom of column thirteen, find a unified, nontechnical, and full account of the news that ought to have been pretty well up in the lead story on page one, namely,

1. How actually does a great nation leave a gold standard, and what is a gold standard, anyway? This is background.

2. What, according to the best of human experience and insight, does it mean? This, of course, is interpretation.

Most of the background facts pertinent to point one may be found in the Times of that day. The lay reader seeking quick access to the heart of the news could have made a good start, in fact, had he read the full text of a statement by the British Government announcing the suspension of gold payments, plus a quotation from the Gold Standard Act of 1925, both of which were on page one. But they were displayed as additions to the news rather than as its core, and so were not given space in the leading story.

To find an interpretation of the event the reader had to wait until the editorial writers, financial men, and specialists got on the job in subsequent days and weeks, although here again he might have made an excellent start by reading Mr. Noyes's financial column in the Times the day the announcement was made. This essential material, however, was printed on page 22 rather than in the news on page one.

If this idea of interpretation in the news goes against the grain of the American newspaper man, who feels in his bones that editorializing must be left to the editorial page though the reader turn to the radio or to the news weeklies, let him remember the individuals he knows personally as laymen and readers. They must remind him of Weber and Field's old story about the saying that barking dogs don't bite: "You know that, and I know that. But the dog—does he know that?" Just so reporters and editors know that news and editorial explanations should never meet. But does the reader, merely skimming the headlines and relying for information on the news weeklies, or tuning in on Boake Carter, act as though he knows it?

I believe that the traditional prejudice of newspaper men against interpretation in the news arose in part, at least, from the fact that it was built up to meet the needs of a simpler world. Did Tippecanoe and Tyler too get the nomination? Did Chicago burn? Did the banker's son seduce a village maiden? To report these things meant simply to recite the facts. Anyone could understand them without help from Walter Lippmann. The only opinion that might exist about them was perhaps a disapproval of Tippecanoe, or of fire, or of the younger generation. It was on these things that what are called the editorial giants of those days let their emotions run loose, and it was better that the news was kept clear of them.

Nowadays, what with the WPA, sit-down strikes, fascism, dust storms, wars that are not wars, the A plus B theorem, silver nationalization, the Comité des Forges, import quotas, Father Coughlin, cosmic rays, nonintervention agreements to screen intervention, and unemployment, news is different. There must be interpretation.

III

The principal change since Tippecanoe's day is that the frontiers of the average man's life, even though he does not realize it, now reach beyond the uttermost horizons known to his fathers. The farmers and business men of previous generations could carry on pretty much as they chose, subject only to near-by influences which they could know and see. But today the welfare of the Kansas farmer depends not only on the rainfall in Kansas, but on Washington and on the rainfall in Argentina as well. It depends on the progress of collectivization and mechanization in Russia. This, with its counterpart in the industrial integration of the world, is an oft-repeated tale. There is no need to go into it, except to note that life is now more complex, more highly integrated with other lives out of sight and even out of ken, than ever before.

It is the effect of this that matters here, in that news sources have become infinitely more numerous and complex. The editor, of course, cannot go completely intellectual. He must still comb the streets for news, via the police, fire-house, hospital, and under-taker. He must assign the usual beats of courts, city hall, hotels, stations, theaters, and Hollywood diaries. But these no longer suffice. News now comes also out of laboratories and books. More disconcerting, it comes out of those human trends and tendencies in the realm of politics and economics and sociology which cannot be charted or measured, and which even the best reporters cannot interview. So it is that, while people still want to read about the big fire downtown and about the Smiths' divorce, they also want to know if Europe has really split again into two armed camps, ready for war.

In sum, then, the journalistic formula being used in preparing the newspaper you will read tomorrow was developed by Pulitzer, Hearst, Stone, and Ochs a generation and more ago. It grew up, literally, with the horse and buggy. Once again it is time to redefine news.

Probably there are as many definitions of news as there are newspaper men. Nevertheless, the reporters, copy readers, and editors of America are in substantial agreement as to what news is, for they all put pretty much the same assortment into their papers. This uniformity springs from a conception of news as the unusual or the spectacular, with particular attention to that trilogy of human interest, action, sex, and money.

When the beginner can recognize this kind of thing, he has a nose for news and has made the first step toward becoming a newspaper man. Thus, during my own first week as a reporter, in Springfield, Massachusetts, one of nine assignments on a given day was to cover a speech by an official of the Northampton hospital for the insane. Pressure of other assignments kept me from hearing the whole talk, which appeared to be an objective summary of contemporary knowledge about mental illness.

It happened that while I was listening the official said something to the effect that 400 persons at large in the county would be confined to the asylum within a year. Here was something spectacular. It was news, and inevitably it found its way into the lead of the story and into the headlines over it. The city editor took occasion to compliment me, the beginner, on having a nose for news; and doubtless many a citizen enjoyed the item at breakfast next morning, perhaps commenting that Aunt Kate would surely be among the 400. The story was strictly accurate in fact, yet because of its lopsided emphasis it gave an inaccurate picture of the event it reported.

For a demonstration of how much more readable background and interpretation can be than even spectacular spot news, one should turn to the files of The New York World reporting the life and times of Celia Cooney, the bobbed-haired bandit of 1924. Here was a sensational crime story, with a cumulative interest built by holdups, shooting, and mystery, climaxed by capture and conviction. Then came publication of a report by Marie Mahon, probation officer, on the young woman's life. It consisted of facts, "marshaled

in smart, orderly fashion," but facts dug out of the human depths
so often passed by in the hurry for news. This report was background of the purest gold. On top of it came an editorial in the
World, written with a stinging realization of the social significance
of the girl's sordid, tragic life. This was interpretation. Revealed
in these three aspects—spot news, background, and interpretation—Celia Cooney's career was more fascinating than the World's
Series, Adolf Hitler, and the quintuplets rolled into one.

IV

Omissions of real news like that, omissions prompted by respect
for the news formulas of Dana's day, may be found on almost any
newspaper page. These omissions run from trivial ones to others
whose ramifications touch obscure corners of modern life where
even experts cannot penetrate. An example is this story from The
New York Times of June 20, 1934:

LEAGUE GIVES LETICIA
BACK TO COLOMBIA

All is Quiet in the Region Over
Which that Nation Nearly
Went to War with Peru

Special Cable to The New York Times

BOGOTA, June 19.—The League of Nations commission transferred
Leticia to the Colombian civil authorities today in brief ceremony.

Conditions in Leticia were reported to be normal and no trouble was
expected.

By the Associated Press

BOGOTA, June 19.—The handing back today to Colombia of the
jungle area of Leticia followed an agreement reached at Rio de Janeiro
between representatives of Colombia and Peru.

The question of sovereignty over the region which had been ad-
ministered by a League of Nations commission for the last year nearly
caused war between those two nations.

The ceremony, as announced here, began at 10:30 A.M. and consisted of an exchange of speeches between General Ignazio Moreno of Colombia, Intendant of the Amazon Territory, and Commissioner Giraldez of Spain on behalf of the League of Nations, followed by the signing of the act of delivery.

Presentation of this bit of news in two items, one a cable from the Times string correspondent in Bogota and the other from the Associated Press man there, offers an obstacle to the smooth absorption of the news by the reader. If the reader is to have first consideration, such items should be rewritten into a single story, without date line or indication of its source at all except the necessary credit to the press association, which might be decently buried in the middle of a paragraph. This is contrary to the usual press association rules. Yet, if the press associations are thus given credit for the news they transmit, surely they should not object to the rewriting of their dispatches to serve that sometimes forgotten man, their ultimate consumer.

If news were so rewritten, the event noted above could be transferred from the jungles of Leticia to the mind of the reader with less effort and more pleasure on his part. It is the news which interests him, not the fact that the story came through the Times man or the Associated Press staff or both. Nor does he like to bite his news off in separate chunks, even though a copy reader has smoothed the way as best he may under the mores now in force on the desk.

V

Sometimes, even today, newspapers will let a rewrite man smooth out the product of scattered reporters handling different angles of the same story. Thus on the morning of August 10, 1934, The New York Herald Tribune had on page one a story under a Sing Sing date line telling of the electrocution of Mrs. Anna Antonio and two accomplices for the murder of her husband. This story was jumped to the bottom of page nine, at the top of which was a separate story under an Albany date line, telling why Governor Lehman refused executive clemency. The New York Times, in spite of the fact that both reports must have come in by wire around midnight, apparently turned them over to a rewrite man, who wove them together into a connected story without any date line at all, simply telling all the news smoothly and intelligibly. It can be done. But these stories, alas, are conspicuous for their rarity rather than for their frequency.

More important than smoothness achieved by regrouping and rewriting, however, is the fact that the item on Leticia quoted above reports "the mere surface of the stream of life" with a vengeance. The Leticia dispute had made big heads on page one in its day, when war threatened. That was the result of the definition of news as that which is startling and spectacular. But the humble formality of a peaceful transfer of sovereignty, so modestly displayed on an inside page, is even more important than the original threat of war. In a sense it is even more unusual.

Think of all the answers to what and how and why which the item quoted does not give. Both background and interpretation are largely missing. Background would mean placing these little cables more in relation to the information contained in all the similar scattered items that had been published during the previous months of the dispute. To leave the item naked, not clothed in its historical environment, is to invite the reader not to read it at all, because it has little meaning for him. He sees a thousand such unrelated items. No wonder he is bewildered and indifferent. And no wonder he turns to his favorite sports columnist or movie critic for relief, for there he can find the news presented connectedly and intelligibly.

If this Leticia item was not placed in relief against its background of previous happenings, neither was it placed in perspective to reveal its significance. It is not only important that an international dispute, even a minor one, has been settled peacefully; it is also important to tell why and how this happened and what it means.

To print this kind of thing as part of the news, of course, would be to steal a valuable feature from the editorial page. But that is just what is needed. The whole newspaper ought to be one vast editorial page in so far as that page offers elucidation rather than argument. Editorial writers themselves have become a new type of reporter. As the news has become more and more complicated they have had to cease viewing with alarm and begin digging for facts in order to make interpretation possible. But the present editorial page, walled in and separated from the living news on page one, has gone unread by the masses. Take the interpretive editorials out of the splendid isolation of that page, multiply them freely, marry them to the news itself, and you will have new life and new color in the news pages. The news will become more intelligible, more readable. Sometimes the interpretation will even make news, as an occasional dope story written under pressure from the dullness of the day's news does now.

It does not answer, I think, to say that interpretation ought to remain cut off from the news, embalmed in a separate editorial page plus perhaps a Sunday feature section. Readers do not make up their minds impartially on the basis of strictly factual news. They absorb the headline's implication, and likely as not let the segregated editorial interpretation which might invalidate their snap opinion go unread. Today's news, or at least that part of it which comes from the socio-politico-economic front, is one whole with its meaning. You cannot cut the two apart into a news story and an editorial and have them remain alive.

Everything that is advocated here is in essence being done already by the American press. But interpretation and background now have to force their way in through editorials, Washington or Wall Street gossip columns, features, interviews with a professor at the local university, dope stories written in odd hours by the political man, or situations mailed by the United Press man in Shanghai. What is needed is a newspaper which welcomes this whole trend and takes it for its own. The bits of interpretation now scattered through the paper must be synthesized into a whole. The paper must take the entire mass, spot news and dope together, and weld it into a connected, smooth-running, and living account of the day's happenings.

To do all this is to put a new responsibility upon the newspaper.

So long as it sticks to surface fact, it dodges a measure of responsibility. As soon as it allows a staff of specialists to drag in background facts and interpretive opinion, it makes itself responsible for these highly interesting additions. Upon its shoulders rests the obligation not only to report that a noise was heard, but also to determine whether this noise is the crack of doom or only the sound of a popgun.

Under such a plan of action the newspaper would once more pioneer a path into the future. It would add to its marvellous mechanical achievements an even greater measure of human expertness than it now gives. It would give the reader something which today he seeks but does not often find. And so long as it did this with integrity of motive, it would avoid the pitfalls which newspaper men fear when they contemplate mixing news and opinion.

For must we not admit that the important difference between news and opinion is a difference in motive rather than a difference in kind? The meaning of spot news in today's sadly puzzled world is part of the news itself; and, so long as it is written with respect for the Fourth Estate's obligation of objectivity, no newspaper man need fear it. So long as the newspaper interprets news with clean hands and a pure heart, the resulting opinion will remain as untainted as the most superficial of today's spot news stories.

To come at last, then, to a redefinition of news, we find that we must simply let the familiar quartet of what-where-when-why pursue their own way a little farther into the roots of an event. News is the important, unusual, or interesting happening seen as a whole and not only on its surface. If the man bites the dog that is still news. But so is a psychiatrist's explanation as to why he did so.

One is reminded of a line from the Spewack's play, "Clear All Wires." As I recall it, the sensation-seeing hero reporter is told by another character, "People aren't interested in news any more. They want to know what's happened."

Breaking the Page-One Tradition

I

It is usual to consider religion as the human institution most bound by tradition and most resistant to change. A casual survey of the contemporary newspaper, however, leads one to suspect that journalism is at least the runner-up in doing things a certain way because that is the way others have done them before.

Newspapers could, of course, reflect the changing news values outlined in Chapter I of this discussion without a major alteration in their physical appearance. At the same time they might do so more effectively if newspaper format, layout, and typography were re-examined as though they were wholly new. Certainly a simpler and more ordered appearance seems implicit in the tendency of American journalism toward organization of the news on behalf of the reader. Consider, for example, the possibilities in this suggestion made in 1924 by William Allen White:

My feeling is that the headline in the American journal will grow smaller, but that it will become more and more important. So much news in the world is concerning us all that we can only take it in tabloid form. I would not be surprised some time to see a newspaper with the entire front devoted to headlines—a sort of index to the elaborated articles on other pages.

A front page containing only headlines is but one of many possible innovations in the physical appearance of the American newspaper. Another is the thoroughgoing classification of all news into departments, along the lines of recent changes by The Palm Beach Times, The Daytona Beach Morning Journal, and The Richmond Times-Dispatch, although here again further typographical changes might be desirable. Only a beginning has been made in the use of pictures, as both European practice and the new picture magazines here indicate. Color is still around the corner lately occupied by prosperity, although it is already peeping around that corner at us. Headlines, make-up, and type dress are well under way toward a change once more. Finally, there is the possibility of a new page size.

We now have just two newspaper formats: the normal size and the half-sized tabloid. Why? Standardization of presses and mechanical equipment, yes; advertising mats and syndicated material based on the 12-em column; paper sizes; and all the rest. Nevertheless newspaper page sizes are accidental offshoots of what happened before, rather than products of a conscious attempt to meet the needs of contemporary living conditions.

Has any publisher in a competitive situation considered how his circulation might benefit if he printed, say, a newspaper half-way between standard and tabloid size, with five 15-em columns set in ten-point type, with a layout based on no consideration other than producing a paper that would be desired and eagerly bought? There are, to be sure, ample material difficulties in the way of such a venture. But granted that the end is desirable and profitable, when has it sufficed in this country to point to the obstacles, shrug one's shoulders, and go on in the same old way?

II

Mr. White's conception of a newspaper front page made up entirely of headlines is not visionary. It has already been approximated by a paper which keeps its feet very much on the ground and which has a larger circulation than any other in the country— The New York Daily News. When the Hauptmann verdict for the murder of the Lindbergh baby was announced, the News abandoned its own formula calling for a first page of pictures and came out (Feb. 14, 1935) with a front page containing nothing but these four words in huge type:

BRUNO GUILTY
—
MUST DIE

That page, in other words, was given over to a single headline. From time to time the News does the same thing, as when it announced the coming of war in Ethiopia in letters four inches high: "War Begins: F. D. R. Pledges Peace for U. S." But the News approached still more closely a front page of headlines serving as a bill of fare for the rest of the paper when it reported the results of the elections of November 6, 1934 (see illustration on page 105). In that issue it gave three-quarters of its first-page space to headlines and the remaining space to bulletins which were themselves hardly more than headlines.

To use the front page to tell all the news, instead of playing up less than a dozen stories on it, offers an infinite variety of combinations. These combinations, however, all lie between two extremes. One extreme is a front page containing nothing but large headlines. This arrangement, presumably ever more fearful and wonderful than a circus poster in appearance, would display a skeleton of the news, but would leave the reader ignorant of essential details. The other extreme is a front page containing no headlines in the accepted sense at all, but a mass of small type giving the news in summaries of sixty or fewer words, like those now used in The New York Times and other large offices to enable editors to keep track of the news while the day's paper is in the process of production.

If these informal bulletins are useful in telling editors quickly and conveniently what the news is, they are presumably useful to readers for the same purpose. Therefore a front page full of them would be ideal from the point of view of presenting all the news quickly. But it would look duller than the front page of The London Times and would repel all but the most determined readers.

Somewhere between these two extremes a useful and stimulating front page must lie.

Here again, as in the interpretation of news, The Richmond News Leader is a pioneer. On April 1, 1935, it began publishing in column one, page one, a digest of the day's news, containing about twenty-five paragraphs averaging twenty-five words each and summarizing the leading stories displayed both on the first page and inside. This one-column digest is presented as a separate feature and is in no sense an index to the paper. Yet it approaches the subject under discussion more closely than the more general summaries and interpretations of the news, like, for example, that of Cleveland Rogers in The Brooklyn Daily Eagle, in that it gives the reader a specific summary of the more important or interesting things that have happened.

A possible disadvantage in the News Leader's arrangement may be noted, however, in that it repeats on the first page the news also told in half a dozen or more first-page headlines and stories. Thus it may happen with this arrangement that the same news appears three times on the same front page—once in the digest, again in a headline, and a third time in the story itself.

More recent innovations along this line are those of The Wisconsin State Journal and The Boise Capital News. The State Journal runs on its first page two features in single-column width, about seven inches long, headed "On the Inside" and "They Say Today." Both have cuts in them. The first contains headlines telling the news of important inside stories plus an index to the departments in the paper. The second consists of lively, brief quotations from persons figuring in the important news stories displayed inside.

The Boise Capital News draws even closer to the first page which gives nothing but a unified, bird's-eye view of the news plus an invitation to read the inside. Most prominent on page one is a varied arrangement of news pictures. Next most noticeable are two double-column bulletins. One summarizes briefly "The News Today" with page references to leading stories, which appear inside instead of in the customary front-page display. The other contains news bulletins received too late for detailed treatment inside. The rest of the page consists largely of a local column plus a number of the brief news stories usually found on page one of an afternoon paper. Saxton E. Bradford, the editor, says in a letter:

We have met with an encouraging response from both readers and advertisers in presenting our news in this manner. Although we have not yet conducted a real survey, voluntary comments are frequent and favorable.

We do not consider that we have perfected our medium. It is a first step toward practical condensation of unimportant news and tabulation of important news. Its advantages to the reader are obvious: its advantages to the advertiser lie in the fact that page one news is now inside next to the ads.

As you see, our page-one style combines elements that have been in operation in other newspapers. Some are purely our own. Our intent is to combine the best practice in news presentation, moving a step beyond into production of a brilliant and thoroughly readable paper that we hope will replace the stodgy newspaper of the past. My personal belief is that only in this way can we keep up with other media.

III

A courageous paper might, I think, gain an advantage over both newspaper competitors and other advertising media by going even farther. One possibility is adoption of a page-one formula providing that, no matter what the exact typographical arrangement chosen, all the news from anywhere in the paper must always appear on page one in adequate summary, to the exclusion of detailed news stories. Even though comics and features are given credit to the full, fundamentally the thing that sells newspapers is news. What better way to present news is there than to put it all on an attractive first page, departmentalized according to subject matter for the convenience of the reader?

There is a vast difference between the ten-word summaries now used in news indices like those in The New York Times, Herald Tribune, and Daily News, and twenty- to sixty-word summaries.

The latter tell the story in detail sufficient for the reader to grasp its meaning and to feel he knows what has happened. Eight- to ten-word summaries are too skeletonized to give this satisfaction.

With a first page made up of bulletins like that, the reader can absorb all the news without once leaving the first page to fight his way through the paper. Then he can read the full story of happenings that interest him on the inside pages, where it would be condensed and interpreted as suggested in Chapter I.

Page one must not only tell all the news, but it must look alive and interesting. This effect can be achieved by several devices. First, headlines must be worked in to give the accustomed highlights of the day at a glance. Next, a fresh, unstandardized layout would break away from the eternal sameness of the American front page. Here at least, where advertising is so rare, there is no barrier to breaking away from the same old eight columns of twelve ems each. There should be a judicious use of white space, achieved by such means as the now almost popular heads set flush at the left plus perhaps indented initials under them. To add interest and make possible a more attractive layout there should also be on page one the outstanding news picture or pictures of the day.

It is obvious that a front page devoted exclusively to a round-up of all the news would have to be broken up into classifications and departments. Just what categories should be chosen, of course, would be a problem for the particular paper undertaking it. The following, however, appear to provide a normal basis for selection (a more detailed list of departments is given in Chapter VII):

Major departments, to take most of the available space: local news, telegraph news, cable (foreign and special) news, and sports.

Minor departments, to take perhaps only an inch in a wide column: markets, financial news, obits, society, books, theater, screen, and weather.

The latter group, being so highly compressed, could vary little from day to day. Now and again, perhaps, a half-inch weather summary would allow an inch and a half for markets on an active day in Wall Street. But by and large there would be relatively little variation in the size of these groupings. The others, however, that is to say local, telegraph, cable, and sport news, could vary as now with the volume of the day's news. If another Armistice should come along, to take an extremely lopsided news day, cable news would get most of the page-one space. But local news would still be there, even though compressed into two inches. And so would yesterday's big wedding or football game and all the rest be there, if in even scantier proportions. For if there is merit in the idea at all, the essential flexibility in displaying news could not be permitted to infringe upon the principle of having all the news on page one. And if the total volume of advertising and news made an unusually large or small paper, the summaries on page one would have to be compressed or expanded accordingly.

If it is argued that adequate summaries of all this material cannot be crowded into a standard-size page, let alone a three-quarter size or tabloid page, I can answer only that experimentally I have done it. An experimental dummy of five fifteen-em columns set in nine-on-ten point type, which was prepared this spring at the Graduate School of Journalism, showed on page one most of the news from The New York Herald Tribune of March 3, 1937.

Incidentally, the reader would bless the newspaper if in preparing page one the practice of leading out the first few paragraphs to make the column fit were eliminated as far as practical necessity allowed. This method permits speed, but it is likely to make the bottom three-quarters of the page appear cramped. A page which offered a type adequately but evenly leaded from top to bottom of the column would be more readable than its competitors. In order to achieve this ideally simple and attractive presentation of the news on page one, to be sure, the copy would have to be written to fit, and an item or two would have to be reset in order to avoid extensive recourse to the devices of leading the first paragraphs and leaving off the last ones. Here some meticulous system of ruled copy paper like that used by the Technology Review might not only pay for itself in composition costs but save endless time as well.

IV

A first page of the kind outlined above, with the usual front-page stories inside, will have the disadvantage of not giving on the front page the details of eight or nine leading stories. But it will more than atone for this by making possible quick and easy absorption of the complicated news of this complicated world. It will banish that newspaper reader's constant annoyance, the page-one story jumped, just when he is getting interested, to some unknown spot in the acreage within.

There is, moreover, another advantage to this method which should appeal to every editor and publisher who is concerned over the distrust of newspapers so frequently voiced by laymen. Does not a part of this hostility spring from a feeling that newspapers do not always reflect accurately the relative importance of news? Before me I have, for example, The New York Times and The Herald Tribune of October 23, 1936. The Herald Tribune gives prominent page-one display—above the fold and on the right—to the story announcing Lewis Douglas's support of Landon in the election. This item does not appear at all on the front page of the Times. It is on page 19.

In the same two papers on October 26, again, appears a similar contrast. The Times leads off with this head in the upper right-hand corner of page one:

'PAY CUT' WARNINGS
ON PENSIONS ISSUE
ASSAILED AS DECEIT

The story reports a statement on this point by the acting head of the Social Security Board. But The Herald Tribune makes no mention on page one of what was the leading story in the Times. Its story is on page 6, under the head:

SOCIAL SECURITY
IN SPOTLIGHT AT
CAMPAIGN'S END

The rest of the headline and the first two paragraphs of the story make no mention of the Social Security Board statement. The story is all there, but because of our present page-one formula many Herald Tribune readers must have missed entirely an important item in the campaign.

This disparity of news emphasis means that readers continually hear later about news events which they did not see at all in their paper because they were buried inside. Is this not inevitable so long as the first page is devoted to a selection from the news, rather than to all of it? Some dull Monday there is a big head on a page-one financial story. Three days later an equally important follow story on the same event gets a small head on the financial page because of the pressure of other spot news on page one. No wonder the reader feels that the paper tells him the news with a false emphasis.

The success of the entire plan suggested here will depend considerably upon the understanding and skill with which both page one and the inside are put together. If the reader really feels that, having read the first page, he gets the essence of all the day's news, he will be satisfied with it. And if he finds the information, background, interpretation, and entertainment he seeks inside, he will buy and read again tomorrow.

News in Perspective

I

THERE IS TODAY a widespread skepticism on the part of newspaper readers as to the objectivity of American news reporting and news display. Although this skepticism is of longer standing than the last election campaign, it was thrown into sharp relief by it, particularly after the votes were counted. For while a large majority of newspapers had supported Governor Landon, a comparable majority of voters preferred President Roosevelt.

From this fact it is now widely argued that the American press is not on the side of the people. This may or may not be true, for we still have no means of telling whether the ultimate interest of the country lay in the re-election of the President or in the election of his opponent. What is of importance, however, is the effect of this split between publishers and public on the standing of journalism as a whole. For whether popular skepticism as to honesty in reporting and presenting news arises from political blood pressures, from direct access to news events through the radio, or from causes as yet unidentified, the fact remains that it does exist.

Therefore it is useful to inquire whether current tendencies toward a change in news presentation might lessen whatever public distrust of the press there is. One possibility was mentioned in the previous chapter; and it is the purpose of the present chapter to explore the details of that possibility.

It is the theory of American journalism that news and opinion are separate. Happenings far and near are reported objectively on the news pages, while political and social opinions are confined to the editorial pages or to editorials, cartoons, and features on other pages which are clearly identified and distinguished from the factual reports of news events contained in headlines and stories. That this theory leads to reporting far more honest than that of continental Europe is obvious. Yet because of what happened in the 1936 election, American newspaper men have been asking themselves whether the American theory is put into practice with sufficient determination to assure to newspapers a strong hold on their readers.

A few weeks before his death Marlen Pew wrote in Editor & Publisher, "I hazard the guess that out of 1,950 daily newspapers the candidacy of Franklin D. Roosevelt is supported by fewer than 700 newspapers. The Republican candidate, Governor Landon, is probably being supported by more than 1,200 daily newspapers."

That was in September. By election day it had become customary to say that 80 percent of the American press opposed the President. If rural weekly newspapers are included, this is probably an underestimate. But for the dailies alone Mr. Pew's figure, which comes to about 35 percent for Roosevelt, seems more accurate. There are 527 dailies listed in Editor & Publisher's yearbook as permanently Republican or Independent Republican, as against 481 Democratic or Independent Democratic. Seven hundred and ninety-two list themselves as independent, however, and without evidence to the contrary one must presume that enough of these supported Mr. Roosevelt to make Mr. Pew's figure of 35 percent at least a well-informed guess. The popular vote for President, on the other hand, was about 62 percent for Roosevelt.

Apparently, then, while nearly two of every three voters favored Mr. Roosevelt, two of every three dailies fought him. Only one of every three publishers, averaging them all together, expressed the majority sentiment. In so far as this newspaper opposition was confined to the editorial page no one can question its propriety.

It is possible, moreover, that the people were wrong and the publishers right. But even so there were occasions on which editorial
policy influenced news, either in headlining, position, or choice of
subject matter for news stories. And one cannot avoid wondering
what effect this practice, and editorial opposition to the majority
political sentiment, are having on newspapers as a whole.

Chicago is a conspicuous example. Here the four big papers, the
Tribune, Daily News, American, and Herald & Examiner, with
circulations totaling nearly 2,000,000, opposed the New Deal.
Only the young tabloid Times, with a circulation which rose from
228,000 to 278,000 during the campaign year, supported Roosevelt.

The bitterness of the large-paper campaign in Chicago against
Mr. Roosevelt is well known. Arthur Robb wrote at the time in
Editor & Publisher, "The Tribune gave more space to politics during the past three months than any other newspaper in the coun-
try, much of it non-campaign news avowedly hostile to the New
Deal." He says also that Colonel Knox's Daily News almost
leaned backward in its effort to present campaign news impartially.
Again, The Chicago Tribune made this editorial comment on the
day after election: "There is one group of his supporters to which
Mr. Roosevelt does feel himself indebted, both for ideas furnished
him and for votes delivered to him . . . It is to men of the stripe of
Dubinsky, Antonini, LaGuardia, Norris and Lundeen, if not at
once to Browder, that Mr. Roosevelt will turn for counsel." And
the mob anger at newspaper men on the occasion of the President's
Chicago speech has generally been credited to the anti-Roosevelt
stand of the big Chicago papers.

II

In Chapter II a policy of devoting page one largely to adequate
summaries of all the news in a daily newspaper was suggested. It
was argued that such a plan might help in counteracting any lack
of faith there may be in newspaper integrity. For such a method

would insure a reasonably equal display of all the day's news, whether or not any particular item happened to favor the editorial position of the paper reporting it. Under the present page-one formula there must be a selection of news for display there. This procedure makes it inevitable that a dozen or more news events receive more prominence in relation to those inside than they merit intrinsically. And it is enough to refer any newspaper man to his own reading of papers far and near during the campaign to indicate that, more often than was desirable, page one was achieved not because of inherent news value so much as because of the paper's political preference.

If, then, a front page consisting chiefly of news summaries would provide a further means toward impartial reporting, it might have business-office value both directly in maintaining circulation and indirectly in furthering reader confidence, which of course makes a paper more effective as an advertising medium. But just how could such a page be prepared?

A page full of paragraphs summarizing the day's grist of news, set in uniform type and displayed one after another, would as noted previously make a repellingly dull news display. Therefore some arrangement of headlines to give the accustomed highlights of the news at a glance is essential. Probably also news pictures and a typographic style allowing enough white space to give light and air would help make a more attractive page. Incidentally, the editor who allows himself to forget newspaper habit and to experiment with various combinations of these elements will encounter arrangements more pleasing to the eye and inviting to the reader than many of today's orthodox front pages. But these details are best left to individual experimentation. (See illustration on page 99.) What is necessary in order to examine the news-summary idea is actual copy. Accordingly a sample is presented in Section IV of this chapter.

This sample is based on the news summaries of a group of related stories used but not published, in accordance with daily routine, in making up The New York Times of October 24, 1936.

They have been changed somewhat to adapt them to their present purpose; for here they are used not to tell editors what news is coming for tomorrow morning's paper, but to give the reader in orderly and concise form a perspective on what happened yesterday.

The particular batch of New York Times summaries from which the samples were chosen happens to be number forty-one. It is by no means a complete set for present purposes, because the late city edition prepared from them—and that was on a Saturday, with a correspondingly thin paper—contained twenty-one other general news stories displayed under top heads, for which summaries were not available. In addition, if the front page is really to give a complete perspective on this particular day's news, one must reckon in also nineteen sports stories; seventeen on business, markets, finance, and related matters; four each for obituaries and society; and six miscellaneous ones like weather, shipping, and book or moving picture reviews—all of which received top heads or comparable display in the paper under consideration.

Even including all these, however, there would be only 103 summaries in all necessary to give a complete preview of everything of any note in that day's paper. At an average of fifty words a summary, which should be ample to allow 100 or more words for leading stories, this makes 5,150 words in all, or about five and a half unleaded columns in the Times's body type. Hence there remains ample room for headlines and pictures, as well as for possible expansion when the volume of advertising or news calls for a bigger paper.

There is, moreover, a possible economy of space as well as a service to the reader in combining related stories into a single summary. Thus five separate stories on various happenings in the Spanish civil war might be summarized adequately in a single bulletin of 150 words, instead of the 250 words which five separate summaries of adequate length would require. There is, in short, enough leeway to open the possibility of using a larger body type, with wider columns, for the kind of front page under consideration. There would be, of course, no stories whatever jumped from page one.

In preparing the sample summaries presented in Section IV, below, which are all concerned with national or state politics, another departure from newspaper habit was made. Here and there a certain informality or simplicity of phraseology occurs, in the belief that a less formal approach makes things easier for the reader. Is it not a common touch in language, for example, that helps make the editorials of The New York Daily News as effective as they are? Or consider by way of further example the following news summaries, published with others in a front-page box headed "The European Crisis" by The New York World-Telegram:

PARIS.—All Europe except three of Germany's war-time allies and countries whose policy is traditionally neutral flock to France's side in consequence of Hitler's scrapping of the Locarno pact. Meanwhile France rushes troops to the border and sends formal protest to the League.

LONDON.—Britain promises military aid to France and Belgium if they are attacked by Germany, but also agrees to consider Hitler's proposal for new treaties; Prime Minister Baldwin presses for action on Britain's $1,500,000,000 rearmament program.

Is not the unstudied directness of that kind of thing more suited to telling the news than the orthodox form of the American newspaper lead, which includes not only the four W's but also several lungfuls of additional information, down to "it was learned in authoritative circles tonight?"

III

There remains also the possibility of a further departure from the present standard. Thus far it has been taken for granted that a front page of news summaries would consist only of a condensed version of the spot news. With certain Washington and foreign and perhaps even local stories, it might be desirable to include added material. The need for this kind of thing has been indicated by the background paragraphs of related material originated by The

Washington Star. Chapter I discussed this point, that background
and interpretation are an integral part of the news.

At least one may say this: if readers desire more background
and interpretation with their news, as there are many signs that
they do, this material belongs in the summaries along with the spot
news. There is an obvious danger in mixing what might often verge
on opinion with straight news. Yet one wonders whether if this
were done with integrity of motive and with scrupulous respect for
the obligation of impartial reporting it would be as dangerously
partial as the kind of news and headlines printed by some papers
during the campaign.

A further question is whether a front page of news summaries
would be expensive in time or money. Since the Times and other
newspapers already produce a goodly portion of these summaries
every day for other purposes, by the simple process of requiring
each reporter or desk man to write a summary of the story he is
working on, they could be prepared in volume with little added
effort. They could be edited, rewritten, cut or expanded as necessary by any copy reader, or preferably by a man delegated especially to the task. And since they would all be set in reasonably
uniform type-size and measure, they would cause little trouble in
the composing room. They would take time on the machines, of
course, but that could be more than compensated for by less headline setting and greater condensation of the news stories inside.

IV

Below are sample front-page news summaries of the type discussed in this chapter. They include all leading national and state
stories on the political campaign which appeared in the New
York Times of October 24, 1936, a date chosen at random.

There are eleven summaries totaling about 630 words. They
cover fifteen stories from the Times of that day, five of which were
given front-page space but ten of which the reader did not discover until he went through the inside pages. The sample summaries follow:

ROOSEVELT. The President, in an address broadcast from Washington to business men attending Good Neighbor League dinners in various cities last night, reiterated his belief in the profit system and private enterprise. No one else has done more to preserve it, he declared. Secretary Morgenthau, addressing the dinner at the Waldorf here, said the stability of the dollar was recognized all over the world. Government revenue does not yet show the real increase to come, which will aid early balancing of the budget. Page 5. . . . The President plans four more major campaign speeches, including one at the Statue of Liberty Wednesday and one in Brooklyn Friday. Page 6.

LANDON. As he traveled through Oklahoma yesterday, Governor Landon in a rear-platform speech at Tulsa indignantly denied the charge of James Roosevelt, the President's son, that 458 schools in Kansas had been closed under his administration. In a speech at Oklahoma City he appealed to "real Democrats" to follow John W. Davis and Alfred E. Smith in voting Republican. He charged President Roosevelt with deserting Democratic principles in an attempt, without mandate of the people, to change the American form of government. Page 5.

PAY ENVELOPES. Industrial employers in Detroit, working with the Republican National Committee, are putting into pay envelopes warnings of an automatic wage cut under the Social Security Law. This is a move to turn Middle Western labor votes from the New Deal. In Washington, Labor's Non-partisan League charged a widespread effort along these lines to force a Landon vote, while in Pittsburgh the Duquesne Club denied Senator Guffey's charges of coercion of its employee vote. Page 7.

DIGEST POLL. The semi-final report of the Literary Digest poll shows Landon still ahead, holding the popular vote at about 11 to 8 and the Electoral College 370 to 161 in the 2,000,000 votes recorded. Special polls of Philadelphia and Pittsburgh show Roosevelt leading, but his margin in Chicago is slight. Page 8.

BLEAKLEY-LEHMAN. The Republican candidate for Governor said in Syracuse last night that heavy taxes would be necessary to balance the state budget, which nevertheless he would balance. Governor Lehman in Rochester asked ratification of the Child Labor Amendment and challenged Judge Bleakley and other Republicans to say where they stand on this issue. He made a labor speech in a strong American Labor Party city, charging that the Republicans want a moratorium on labor legislation. Page 8.

ONEIDA COUNTY. Utica appears lost to the Republicans this year, but because its vote is normally less than half that of the total for Oneida

County, the rural sections appear able to roll up a majority big enough to carry the county for Landon and Bleakley by from 3000 to 6000. Page 8.

CONGRESS. Chicago Republican officials say they expect to control the next House if Landon wins, and to gain at least 100 more "sure" seats even if Roosevelt is re-elected. Page 9.

CAMPAIGN FUNDS. The Republican National Committee has received $4,038,319 and spent $4,949,428 from June 1 to October 18. William R. Hearst, with $30,000, tops the contributors' list. Page 9.

REGISTRATION. New York State registrations will reach an all-time high of more than 6,150,000, an increase of 15 percent over 1932. Table of registration by counties. Page 10.

MAINE. Senate investigators of campaign expenditures report thousands of Maine voters threatened with disqualification at the polls because they are on relief. Complaints said the Republican Attorney-General used an old pauper law for this purpose. Page 10.

J. EDWARD JONES, dealer in oil royalties now under Federal fraud indictment, yesterday accused the Democratic National Committee of offering to get him out of his trouble in return for a $2500 contribution. Page 10.

Is not news in this form easier to grasp than the usual assortment scattered through the paper?

The Specialist in the News Room

I

IN A RECENT TALK ON FOREIGN NEWS before a meeting of Associated Press managing editors in Chicago Arthur J. Sinnott, editor of The Newark Evening News, put his finger on something which is troubling newspaper readers.

The big problem today is to evaluate foreign news. . . . [he said].
It may be that an occasional special, pulling together the developments of a week or month, would help greatly to give meaning to international developments. I find that I can get a lot more out of an occasional magazine piece or Sunday feature than I can from the day-to-day copy. And if we have difficulty, what must the public have?

The question Mr. Sinnott asks about foreign news may be asked also about national news and news of economics, science, or similarly complex matters. The newspaper reader's difficulties with this kind of news, which is more and more forcing its way into the papers, has given rise to this book. It is based on the premise that now as in the past social changes are forcing technical changes on newspapers; in particular, that readers are ready for a greater organization of the news than they now get.

With this in mind previous chapters have discussed the possibility of including more background and interpretation with the news, of devoting the front page to adequate summaries of all important stories throughout the paper, and of departmentalizing general news as well as news of sports, finance, society, and the other specialties.

Granted that these physical changes in the newspaper are desirable, what office changes would have to be made to realize them? The central factor in these changes was pointed out, I think, by Mark Ethridge, general manager of The Louisville Courier-Journal and Times, when he said last year:

I believe that there will be a major mutation in the style of news handling within the next few years. My own idea . . . is that instead of having a central copy desk the medium-sized newspaper will have a copy desk of specialists. As the news comes in it will be channeled to various men who have the background and the knowledge of how to handle it. They will take all the grist of the day's mill and fit it into connected stories that are both comprehensible and interesting.

It goes without saying that the problem varies with the size and situation of the individual paper seeking to meet it. On a fairly large paper which devoted page one to a summarized perspective on all the news and which departmentalized its general news, the mutations of which Mr. Ethridge speaks might take the following forms:

1. Development of a research department, to be of first-rank importance in the office
2. Merging the tasks of rewrite men and copy readers
3. A separate rewrite desk devoted to page one
4. A resultant method of routing copy through the office slightly different from that usual in the news room

II

The growth of the research department is already well under way. In Editor & Publisher's fifty-year jubilee issue (July 21, 1934) Maurice Symonds, librarian of The New York Daily News, pointed out that the musty and haphazard morgues of former days are giving way to highly organized and ambitiously equipped libraries. But to realize the objectives advocated here further steps in the direction indicated by Mr. Symonds are necessary.

A promotion letter from Fortune magazine, for example, boasts that

Fortune articles are not written—they are rewritten. On the average, twelve to fifteen people are intimately concerned with the researching, writing, editing, and checking of each Fortune manuscript. A total of more than 8000 editorial hours were charged against one monumental Fortune summation before the editor was satisfied that he had himself pounced on every inconsistency; that the writers had glossed over no essential point; that the checkers had verified every statement. All of which suggest that Fortune's staff is large. It is—four editors, fourteen writers, twenty-two assistants and fourteen college-trained researchers whose job is to deluge the writer with facts and to guarantee the correctness of each sentence in his completed manuscript.

Make as many allowances as you wish for the differences between magazine and newspaper work; deduct as much as you like for the ebullience of promotion men when they advertise their wares; and still there remains an editorial method which might be more useful to newspapers than it is: namely, the joint writing or rewriting of stories based not only on spot news but also on related background or interpretive material.

Not long ago The New York World-Telegram published a story about a municipal employe who was sentenced to two years in prison for accepting bribes. Instead of letting it go at that the Telegram used in the story facts from a probation report on the man. It was this report that made the story worth the page-one display it got. Without it the story was routine. With it the story became a fascinating human document.

The point need not be labored, because it is familiar. Yet it is well to ask whether enough use is made of this practice of digging under the surface of the news in order to get the full value from it. Newspapers make great efforts to dig up news outside the office; but do they dig up its background once they have it, either outside, as with the story just cited, or inside when it is a question of reference material?

The form a newspaper research department might take is difficult to specify without a particular office in mind. It is certain, however, that if a research department is to be a means toward producing good copy it ought to be more than a morgue plus the usual reference library. It should have not only clippings, speeches, pamphlets, official texts, reports, dissertations, source-books, and other printed matter but something far more important, human resources in the way of one or more individuals trained in research. It requires no great stretch of the imagination to visualize a future big-city newspaper's research department comparable to that of the Foreign Policy Association or the Brookings Institution.

III

With an organization like that, even if of modest size, the elements of background and interpretation so often missing in the news stories of today would find their way regularly into the paper. But it is still necessary to provide for greater organization of the news on behalf of the reader. With many a story—those which are not run-of-the-mine straight narratives, like fire or accident stories—this would mean rewriting the spot news to get in added facts from the research department, or to combine two or more stories into an intelligible whole.

It is the desirability of providing a smoothly-functioning machinery for this purpose that leads to the suggestion of merging the tasks of copy reader and rewrite man. Essentially the change means simply fewer men on the desk and more on rewrite. On a small newspaper this rewrite battery for general news might consist of a single desk, while on larger papers it would be divided into separate desks devoted to cable, telegraph, and local news. Were this larger paper fully departmentalized, the rewrite-and-copy desks might be subdivided by subject-matter, each desk handling one or more departments.

Whatever the size or arrangement of the office, the men who handle news in this fashion ought to specialize in editing their subject matter. They ought not to be experts in the sense of being authorities on their subject, however, because that kind of thing is likely to result in stuffy, unreadable copy. Whatever expert authority is needed to supply background and interpretation for a story ought to come from the research department, leaving to the rewrite-copy desk or desks only the job of producing concise, intelligible copy. It would be their duty to take the spot news as it comes in, to read it with the eyes of the uninformed reader, and then edit or rewrite it to the extent needed. They would take nothing for granted, whether an obvious legal phrase in a story from the courthouse beat or an abstruse scientific bit from the research department. They would ask again the questions why and how and what, in reference to even the simplest things, and answer them.

Many a story obviously must go through the present routine from reporter to desk to composing room, especially if it is near the deadline. But others, if they deal with the higher realms of economics or celestial mechanics or what not, would benefit from the ministrations of a good rewrite man who had been given also the job of copy reader, of getting the story into its final shape, with adequate support from a research department.

With the functions of copy reader and rewrite man thus merged in order to organize the news for the reader, the reporter remains, as always, the backbone of the news machine. But the combination of rewrite plus copy-reading plus research will produce a kind of reporting which the reader seeks more often than he finds. He will be more likely to get all the news rather than only its superficial aspects. Stories produced by this method should transport the reader to the scene of action, let him see it, and tell him what it means—all in a simplified, unified, and orderly copy.

In company with the other points put forward in these pages this suggestion is not fundamentally different from what is being done in the well-organized news rooms of today. The combined rewrite-and-desk men, though the emphasis of their tasks might be a little unaccustomed, are hardly different from what a good rewrite man is today. The only difference is that there would be more of them, that they would have research assistance when that is needed, and above all that they would be given a freer hand in rewriting or editing copy.

IV

If copy reader and rewrite man are to become one, who is going to have time to write heads? Perhaps the answer is that just as space can be saved by rewriting two or more separate stories (for example, telegraph and local angles) into a single account, so time can be saved by wasting less of it on heads. John E. Allen, editor of The Linotype News, writes that "We have kept no list of papers that have adopted simplified heads, but I know that such papers run into the hundreds." Some papers have scrapped half the banks and crosslines they used to use, and others have adopted the flush-at-left heads which not only lessen the need for awkward phraseology but also free the desk from the time-wasting bonds of the unit count.

It is reasonable to ask whether this tendency may not be carried even farther. If the head identifies the story as to subject and extent, is that not enough? Or must the copy reader make the effort and take the time to tell the reader in outline everything that the story itself contains? If the copy itself is already checked and put into final form on a rewrite-and-copy desk, a small universal desk ought to be equal to the task of writing simplified heads for it. Or if it seemed more desirable, the combined rewrite and copy desks could not only prepare copy but write heads as well. This would leave to the universal desk only the tasks of coördinating the day's grist of copy and of preparing page one.

Page one, as discussed on pages 19-27, contains in addition to headlines and pictures, summaries of all stories throughout the paper which now get display under top heads. These summaries would have to be grouped as local, national, foreign, sports, financial, and so forth. So, too, the preparation of these summaries would have to be departmentalized. Taking the advance summaries already in use in some offices, a good rewrite man could smooth them out into an ordered perspective on the days news.

If this task were again subdivided with different men on local, national, foreign, sports, and financial news—or whatever the departmentalized news-categories were—the job would be that much better done.

V

To introduce changes along these lines into the news room might require some rearrangement of office furniture, but the essentials of the news machine would remain the same.

On The Richmond Times-Dispatch (see pages 67-69), the largest paper which to date had adopted departmentalization, the shift was made with a minimum of stress. Under the old system there had been a universal desk consisting of seven copy readers, a slot man, and a telegraph editor. The telegraph editor became the news editor, and all others became editors of particular classifications of news. The news editor sits in the slot and passes out A.P., state, and local copy to the editors, who sit at desks jutting out from the semicircle. The city staff has hardly been disturbed by the change, since it already was a department in itself. By way of meeting the need for a research department, the morgue and its resources were enlarged. In addition each department editor has a filing cabinet, is supplied with reference essentials, and is charged with the further development of his own source material.

In any such change from standard practice the most noticeable departure from customary practice would be that copy, instead of flowing along channels determined by its origin, would follow channels determined by its subject matter.

Under current methods it is possible, if unlikely, for a cable from Paris on the devaluation of the franc plus a related story from Washington on the stabilization of currencies plus another containing the Wall Street angle to be read on the cable, telegraph, and financial desks respectively. As a result they may even appear on separate pages. Certainly the chances are that, being handled by three different groups of men, they will not be so organized and fitted together as to present the whole story in clear perspective to the reader. With the object of clear, concise, and intelligible presentation of the news always in mind, it would seem desirable that these stories should be read and perhaps rewritten as parts of one whole by the financial desk, whose writers, with the help of the research department, would be able to produce a clearly-focused single piece of copy.

The whole subject of emphasis on rewrite, of research workers in the city room, and of changes in office routine is interesting not in itself, but as a means to a more intelligible presentation of news to the reader. After all, further efforts on behalf of the reader might sell more papers.

What Is a Headline?

I

NOTHING IRRITATES THE AMERICAN newspaper reader more than that part of the paper with which he is most familiar, and upon which he relies most heavily for news of what is happening in the world—the headline. Day in and day out the headline gives him the essence of the news, but its swift service is so familiar that the reader hardly notices it. What he does notice are the headline's aberrations in false emphasis and in puzzling or awkward phraseology.

The reader probably does not know that false emphasis, when it occurs, usually arises from the necessity of selecting a lead idea for the headline; and that the phraseology over which he now and again stumbles and halts comes from copy-desk obeisance to the gods of Balance and Unit Count—that is, from making the headline look well typographically and fit the space allotted. If he does know this, however, he probably agrees with J. Roscoe Drummond of The Christian Science Monitor in saying, "It seems almost true that the rules which we have laid down to guide our headline writers have become more powerful than the purpose for which they were originally made."

The puzzled reader of 1937, indeed, might welcome a return to the headline formula of the days of Queen Anne, which led to this characteristic display in a Postscript to The Postman (London) of August 11, 1710:

This Day came in an Express, with the welcome News of a Victory obtain'd by the King of Spain, over the Forces of the Duke of Anjou. Which is in Substance as follows.

That headline tells about the news. Today's headline tells the news itself: "King of Spain Defeats Anjou," or something of the kind, together with more of the who, what, where, when, why of the story, all in the barest minimum of words. This directness, centering in use of an active verb in the present tense, unquestionably makes the headlines more useful to the reader. But while the American headline was developing directness and force, it was also being sent into a typographical concentration camp. The very striving for simplicity and speed, coupled with consideration for typographical appearance, gradually confined the headline within boundaries which all too often do not allow it to tell the news with the easy naturalness of the older style exemplified by the headline quoted from The Postman.

II

It is unnecessary to resurrect classic headline errors like "Jones Will Fight Hinges On Baby," which says one thing and means another, in order to show what this confinement sometimes does to the headline. Anyone's daily reading will reveal defects less glaring but nevertheless irritating. Two recent run-of-the-mine samples from The New York Times, which has headline standards at least as high as any in the country, are: "Teachers Demand All-State Tenure" and "Radio Union Made RCA Bargainers." The lay reader must study the succeeding banks of these heads before he has much of an inkling as to what they mean.

One can find the same kind of thing almost at random in American newspapers, as, for example, in this one from The Chicago Daily News: "Democrats Sure of 7 Governors, Winning 17 More." On the same day the same paper ran this sports head: "Badgers Have Good Record in Upsets." This was perhaps intelligible to football fans, but surely it did not tell the ordinary reader that Northwestern was worried about Wisconsin's penchant for turning in a victory when a defeat is forecast. Again, the tight unit count forced The Chicago American to put into three unrelated headlines on a single page of election news (page 5, issue of November 4, 1936) the contraction Dems in place of Democrats or Democratic Party, thus: "Dems Hold Sure Rule of Assembly; Dems Tighten Control over Congress; and Dems Clinch Congress Seats."

In the eyes of seriously-minded observers of the public scene these sins of phraseology shrink into mere peccadilloes when compared with false emphasis in headlines, for false emphasis may lead to distortion of the news. To turn once more to The New York Herald Tribune and The New York Times, we find these heads over accounts of the same event:

Herald-Tribune:

ALDRICH ASKS
AID FOR 'WISE'
SECURITY ACTS

Times:

ANGELL BIDS NATION
YIELD SOME RIGHTS
TO KEEP DEMOCRACY

In fairness to our present headline formula it must be said that a subordinate crossline and bank in the Times headline said, "Aldrich Warns Business. He Declares It Must Assume Responsibility of Aiding the Common Good." And the last bank of The Herald Tribune head said, "Dr. Angell Predicts Individual Will Surrender More Rights to Majority." Both papers, in other words, tried to live up to the contemporary headline ideal of telling the whole story, namely that both men spoke and that they said in substance thus and so. But one wonders whether rapid readers of the Times and the Herald Tribune that morning did not get sharply different pictures of the same event.

Another headline in the Times—the leading one on December 14, 1936, said "Ex-King and 'Alien' Set Rebuked by Canterbury."

The obvious inference is that the Archbishop objected to Edward's association with Mrs. Simpson because she was a foreigner. The Archbishop, however, had said (according to the Times' own account), "Even more strange and sad is it that he should have sought his happiness . . . within a social circle whose standards and ways of life are alien to all the best instincts of his people." It was the gay way of life rather than Mrs. Simpson's nationality which disturbed the Archbishop. Singling out the word "alien," then, made an inaccurate and misleading headline. The American headline style calls for a concrete, specific statement of the news within the boundaries of the column rules. It is exceedingly difficult to do that and remain accurate. In fact it is amazing, considering the difficulties, that our headlines tell the news as accurately as they do.

III

Considerations like these, together with the further one that many headlines now in use repeat an unnecessary amount of the material told in the story itself, have led many newspapers in recent years to change their headlines. In the main these changes have taken three forms: simply scrapping the bottom parts of the old-style headline; setting heads flush at the left with little regard for balance and unit count; and changing the philosophy of the headline entirely.

Since 1928 John Allen has urged the first two of these changes—setting heads flush at the left and simplifying them—in The Linotype News, of which he is editor. And as most newspaper men know, Earle Martin was a pioneer in introducing them on large newspapers by adopting them in The Cleveland News in 1934. In that paper an eight-column streamer, "Rebels in Mass Attack on Madrid," for example, is followed not by the accustomed typographical display gradually stepping down into the story itself but by this simple two-column hanger: "Hurl Forces Against Capital as Defenders Start Counter Blow." In single-column heads throughout the paper the News has now given up everything but the tops of the orthodox American head. It uses simple three-line arrangements, with all secondary banks omitted, as for example, "Woman Is Held as Auto Victim Is Near Death." This unadorned statement suffices for the headline, and the rest of the news is told where it belongs—in the story.

Mr. Martin's testimony on the results of this experiment, as quoted by J. Roscoe Drummond at the 1935 meeting of the American Society of Newspaper Editors, is this: "It is the only time that I have ever made a type change in a newspaper and received an immediate response from the reader. People who do not have enough technical knowledge of type to understand just what we have done know that the paper is easier to read, and say they like it."

To this Frank O'Neill, head of the News copy desk, adds:

Now that balance is a dead bogey we are able . . . to get to the heart of the story with a maximum of speed and a minimum of arithmetic, i.e., unit counting. The message can be told naturally, as in ordinary speech, without compelling the copy editor to strain for the perfectly balanced combination which the conventional headlines demand. As you know, these balanced combinations . . . require endless juggling and jockeying, and are bound to involve a certain amount of clutter and surplusage. Consequently, they tend to rob the headline of clarity and "punch."

The new headline, limited only by the maximum count, eliminates the clutter and the surplusage because it lets the head tell itself, so to speak. It tosses out the window the stimulants so endlessly demanded to keep the well-dressed head alive. You know—"Get two more units in that second line and make it balance." It has also served to put the bromide on a starvation diet.

Further testimony on the advantages of heads set flush to the left and omitting secondary banks comes from D. D. Mich, managing editor of The Wisconsin State Journal, who wrote in The Quill for September, 1936:

The new headline schedule also saves time for us in the composing room. A linotype machine which formerly was used full time in setting heads now produces all the heads and from two to four columns of straight matter in addition. . . .

We have increased our news space from three to four columns a day by eliminating all secondary banks on headlines.

How many newspapers have simplified their headlines in the last few years no one knows, but the number must run into the hundreds. Some of them go the whole way, as did The Cleveland News; and others, like The Los Angeles Times, retain a subsidiary bank in their major heads.

The third contemporary headline change marks an even further departure from the orthodox type. This is the headline form of which Mr. Hearst has been in the past two years the most aggressive practitioner. His departure resulted from a trip to England and was frankly modeled on the typographical gyrations of the British popular press. It consisted largely of writing captions instead of headlines which tell the news and of displaying them by means of typographical heteorogeneity. When first introduced in 1934 on the first page of the second section, typical heads ran like this:

POLLY'S

DIAMONDS

———

THEY CAME BACK

Or even:

ALL THERE

———

EVEN THE ODORS

More recently the headlines, while retaining a liberal use of capitals and some of the original typographical breathlessness, have in content returned more to the orthodox form. Thus in The New York American, for example, one sees three lines of caps, the middle one in smaller type, saying "Relief Investigators Trial," followed by a bank in lower case which explains, "Allegedly Took $5 to Get Man on Rolls."

Still other changes have been introduced by The Christian Science Monitor and The Chattanooga News. Under Mr. Drummond the Monitor has developed a flexible one-line head, in 24- to 30-point Bodoni with occasional use of italics, which may stretch anywhere from two to six columns. These headlines are admirably adapted to simple, direct, and natural statements of the news, thus: "Winter Sports and Ski Tournament Opens at Boston Garden." This kind of head is used either by itself or else with a brief single-column hanger.

Even simpler are the heads with which The Chattanooga News began to experiment last August. One example consisted of a large italics "War:" leading into a small Bodoni line reading: "America Protests; Rebel Bombs Kill Women; Mussolini Increases Tension." This appeared over cuts and wire copy on the Spanish civil war. The various items making up this copy had separate captions: "Bombardment," "Duce's Boast," and "Forlorn Hope." Apparently these heads did not identify their stories with sufficient clearness, for J. Charles Poe of the News said of the experiment, "We have had some criticism of it and I must confess no commendation."

IV

Most publishers and editors probably agree with Paul Bellamy, editor of The Cleveland Plain Dealer, who said recently, "I am greatly concerned about the position of the newspaper in public estimation."

At the moment public estimation of newspapers may revolve largely about political matters, but year in and year out the daily barrage of headlines must have its effect, both good and bad. Some of the changes and experiments in headlines just noted may help eliminate the bad effects on public estimation. Yet it is arguable, I think, that far more can be done. Ot least one major field of headline experimentation remains: namely, lessening the vast disparity in size between the largest and the smallest heads in the present schedules.

It is a common experience for the reader to be fascinated by a story displayed prominently for a day or two, only to find later that he has missed an interesting follow story the next day, which the pressure of fresh news has caused to be played down. He can hardly complain because the paper has given chief play to fresh news; but he is justified in complaining that the follow story was buried under a head so tiny as to be all but invisible. The effectiveness of this overshadowing of small heads by big ones cannot be doubted. Mussolini and Hitler pay tribute to it every day when, feeling they cannot suppress disagreeable items entirely, they order them displayed inside under microscopic heads. Honest and accurate reporting is a matter not only of printing the news but also of displaying it.

The current American tendency to omit subsidiary banks from headlines has done something to remedy this situation, because shortening the big headlines has brought it down in size a little toward the small one. The disparity between top heads and the smallest in the paper, however, is still too great to permit a balanced display of the news. This indicates that the size of the smallest heads in the schedule might well be increased somewhat so that they can catch the attention of the man whose eyes get a daily battering from 36 point type at the top of the page.

This increase in the size of the smaller heads might well be carried over to include the subheads within a single story. A clipping before me, for example, contains two reports from Rome displayed under a single head of the orthodox kind, which reads "Italy Bans Paper Attacking Britain . . . Ottobre Seized for Proposing Bombardment of Malta—Subsidy is Charged . . . Foreign Writers Warned . . . Are Advised to Send Out Only Such Military Data as Are Officially Given Out."

The two stories under this head contain four items of news: 1. The Italo-Ethiopian conciliation commission held a preparatory session; 2. The Italian newspaper compaign against Britain continued, although the government clamped down on the particularly virulent Ottobre; 3. Foreign writers were warned against using non-official news; and 4. Another Rome newspaper accused Britain of subsidizing Haile Selassie. Under present standards it is difficult to see how a headline noticeably better than the one used could be written. The copy reader succeeded in producing a nicely-balanced head which told the news of two of the four items clearly, and hinted at a third. More than that is pretty much to ask.

This particular headline, however, takes up nearly three inches of the column. If all subsidiary banks were omitted, leaving only 'Italy Bans Paper Attacking Britain," the head would take less than three-quarters of an inch. Why not use some of this saving in space for subheads identifying each of the four items of news? These subheads might be anything up to, say, 18 point. Certainly they could easily be larger than the tiny one-line boldface subheads now used almost universally—not to serve as minor headlines, but merely to break up a mass of type. Why not break the mass up still more and in addition identify for the reader that part of the news that is played down, as well as that which is played up?

V

Possibly a wholly new approach to the function of the headline might get around many of the headline difficulties which still remain. If we could abandon the attempt to have the headline tell in tabloid everything that is in the story and still let the reader get the news quickly, we should have something.

A newspaper of the kind discussed in previous chapters, one which prints on the front page summaries of important stories from throughout the paper, might achieve something of the kind. In order to tell the big news at once the front-page display would have to include something resembling the present standard headline. But because these headlines could break across the column rules they would not be confined by the low unit count which is the lot of the single-column front-page head. These chief headlines of the day might even be segregated by themselves, together with the summaries pertaining to them, in a two-or three-column box.

For the other important stories throughout the paper the front-page summaries, tying the various angles of big stories together into simple, direct statements in plain English, would take the place of headlines. The inside heads would then have a function not unlike that served by inside jump heads now. They would not have to tell the whole story, because that would already be told, in essence, on page one. The inside headlines would merely have to identify the story, and to suggest some of the color or details to be found there.

One may see the thing concretely by taking a standard paper of today and speculating what might be done under such a scheme. The Herald Tribune of December 9, 1936, the day before Edward's abdication, ran this head across five columns: "King and Baldwin Confer for 5 Hours; Solution on a Friendly Basis Is Hinted; Lawyer and Doctor Fly to Mrs. Simpson." Also on page one is a related story saying that the Irish Free State might bar the Duke of York from the throne. Inside are four more major related stories, saying that Mrs. Simpson might visit Rome, giving sketches of the doctor and lawyer who flew to Cannes, telling of the British press reactions, and outlining French political repercussions of this biggest story of the year.

The front-page-of-summaries paper would have on page one a headline much like the one used by the Herald Tribune. It would have also in summary form on page one the main news from other stories throughout the paper. Inside it would have the same color and details as did the Tribune, but it could save considerable space on headlines. The stories printed on the British crisis that day revolved about two centers—King Edward at London and Mrs. Simpson at Cannes. Thus inside there would be two main heads, perhaps single lines spread over several columns as in The Christian Science Monitor, with the other heads and their stories grouped under one or the other of these two. These minor heads, not necessarily displayed at the top of the page as in the Tribune, might be modeled on those seen in many magazines. These are flush-at-the-left heads, which may run either one or two lines, and thus are flexible enough to vary from one to eight or even ten words, depending on the type used.

The main inside heads, then, would merely have to identify their copy as coming from London and Cannes. They might read something like this: "In Britain, a Conference" for one, and "In Cannes, Mystery" for the other. Under the first would be run, at the head of their copy as it happened to fit into the forms, brief heads like the following: "London Press Sees Early End of Crisis," and "Ireland May Keep York from Throne." Under the other main head ("In Cannes, Mystery") might be the minor head "The Doctor and the Lawyer," and "Mrs. Simpson May Visit Rome." A reader aware of the chief developments from page one could easily find his way about with headlines as unorthodox and as brief as these.

All this, of course, raises detailed questions of typography which could be settled only by the paper undertaking such a venture. Meanwhile one may sum up the contemporary American headline by quoting once more Mr. Drummond's admirable statement before the A.S.N.E.: "The English language, rich and brilliant as it is in its expressions and shadings, was not created to live and flower within the confines of a 13-em column or a 12-unit head."

Departmentalizing the News

I

LAY CRITICS OF THE PRESS have long complained that they get a confused picture of the news from our newspapers, and if newspaper men can put themselves in the position of the conveniently objective man from Mars they may agree. For if one forgets for a moment the standards and traditions and habits of American newspaper make-up and news display, one discerns a surprising lack of orderliness in the way in which news is presented to the reader. Consider, for example, the man who became interested in a story about British affairs in his newspaper, and who read on down to this last paragraph:

"The problem of getting a seat or standing room along the coronation route or a glimpse of the new king and queen at one of the great ceremonial occasions during the coming spring and summer is one of the main worries of the loyal British subject."

TOWN REQUIRES
SNAKE OWNERS
TO POST BOND

By United Press.

GETTYSBURG, PA., Jan. 18.—The town council here acted on the petition of a number of housewives and passed an ordinance providing that any person desiring to harbor snakes, rodents, skunks, "or any dangerous and loathsome creatures," must take out a $5 license and post a $500 bond.

The jolt felt by this reader on bumping suddenly into snakes and skunks when his mind was attuned to the pageantry of George VI's coronation is experienced daily by American newspaper readers. The stories quoted here happened to appear in The South Bend Tribune, but so long as American newspapers retain their present methods of make-up and news display, the shift from King George to snakes in the space of a quarter of an inch, and countless similar mixtures of news, can be duplicated in almost any of them.

The American newspaper displays the news by putting over each item a headline which is a tabloid version of the story itself. But there its organization of the news on behalf of the reader all but ceases. The front page, to be sure, is a sort of headline for the whole paper, in the sense that it lifts out of the day's news the most important, interesting, or spectacular stories and presents them at once for the reader's inspection. This practice, however, may be as much of a hindrance as a help to the man who wants to get the essense of the day's news. Playing on page one all sorts of stories which have nothing in common except that they stand out above the rest of the day's supply means that there is grouped together a collection of wholly unrelated items.

The theory is, of course, that the news is clearly identified by its headlines and that by skimming them both on the front page and inside the reader can sample all the news there is. He does not have to wade through each story itself to find out whether he thinks it is worth reading or not. Millions of copies sold and read every day demonstrate the soundness of this theory. It is a question, however, whether the system of selecting, displaying, and organizing the news could not be carried farther. If all the news throughout the paper were grouped into departments containing stories dealing with the same general type of subject matter, the news could be seen in orderly perspective, and some at least of the confusion complained of would disappear.

It is true that on the inside pages of our papers there is a tend-

ency to segregate some of the news into certain broad classifications. Sports, finance, and society, for example, are usually grouped
together in one or more pages. Usually, too, some effort is made to
bring together in one place the local news, the foreign news, and
the national news. Nevertheless these classifications are by no
means rigid, nor are they thoroughgoing. Something of the habits
of page one, with its mixture of the important and the sprightly,
the sublime and the ridiculous, usually carries over to these loose
groupings of the news within. There is nothing to keep the make-up
man from sandwiching an extra local story into a convenient space
in the sports forms, or from putting into adjoining columns on the
general news pages items bearing as little relation to each other as
"British Regency Bill Assailed in Commons" and "2 Women Killed
on New Parkway."

In recent years editors have given signs of dissatisfaction with
the results of this kind of thing, and by means of news indices,
news digests, special-writer columns, and week-end reviews, they
have sought to bring order out of the surrealist headline procession.
The latest indication of this trend is an experiment begun on January 4, 1937, by The Buffalo Times. In the top half of the first page
of the second section the Times now prints summaries of the important news of the day, both wire and local. Individual stories appear under general headings like Nation, Business, Abroad, Medicine, and Labor. The stories are not only concise accounts of spot
news rounded out with background material but, being presented
under department heads, they give the reader an impression of
smoothness and orderliness instead of offering him side by side such
strange bedfellows as "Borah Predicts 6 Arduous Years" and "Girl
Knifed, Father Held."

II

Earlier in this book Stanley Walker was quoted as saying that
Time and The New Yorker had "demonstrated what some people
suspected all along—that facts, marshaled in smart, orderly fashion,
can be charming." And it is chiefly the example of the news week-

lies in thus marshaling facts, whatever their faults in other respects, that has set editors to thinking about thoroughgoing instead of partial departmentalization of the news.

The prospect is stimulating. One visualizes a paper which presents its news in something like the manner in which a metropolitan department store dresses its show windows. If, to put it the other way about, these stores applied to their windows the technique of the front page and of all too many inside pages, we might see something like this:

A display of fine groceries, with choice hams resting on boxes of English biscuits and jars of peanut butter surrounded by smoked herring. Draped over a succulent liverwurst would be a brassiere and a pair of scanties, while a basket of fruit would reveal the protruding barrel of a shotgun. In the next window would be women's fashions for southern wear, tastefully decorated with cans of paint and vacuum cleaners and flanked on one side by mattresses and on the other by velocipedes and whisky bottles.

One need not carry the analogy too far, yet it is hardly more fanciful than the assortment of items appearing on news front pages. We know well what attractive window displays the big stores make, with a carefully arranged composition of men's sports wear in one window, toys in another, and evening dresses, say, in a third. It makes an orderly, harmonious whole which takes on color and sprightliness not only from the goods themselves but also from the harmony and taste with which they are grouped. One wonders if there is any good reason why the day's news should not be similarly organized for the reader.

In these pages I have argued for a front page which, by carrying reasonably detailed summaries of all important news from throughout the paper, would carry still farther the present headline function of page one. This kind of front page would give a bird's-eye view of everything of importance or interest in the paper. If there is merit in departmentalization, this front page should be divided into groups of summaries (national affairs, local news, science, sports, and the like) which match the news departments inside.

In order to squeeze the full advantage from departmentalized news on the inside pages, the major departments should appear in unvarying order day after day, much as the editorial or financial pages are regularly found in roughly the same position now. In other words, no matter how much or how little news there was in them on any given day, and no matter what shrinkage or expansion the advertising schedule might call for, the major departments would always appear in fixed order. Immediately after page one would come local (or natonal or foreign) news, with the others in a familiar order. Thus the reader could easily find his way about—a fact which stimulates reader interest and circulation.

The advertiser, too, ought to like this arrangement of the news. For the biggest stories of the day, though summarized and headlined on the front page, would themselves be scattered throughout the paper as the departmental order determined. This would put a great part of the advertising next to page-one reading matter instead of, as now, back among what is left over.

Any paper adopting this plan would, of course, make up a list of news departments of its own, depending upon its requirements and preferences. Some of the departments, like society, finance, and the major divisions of general news into local, national, and foreign, would appear in all papers every day. Others of less universal interest would appear when the news warranted and space considerations permitted.

Sometimes the pressure of news development might force new and temporary classifications into the paper. The 1937 floods of the Ohio and Mississippi, a political campaign, a crisis in the Spanish war, or a national convention of the American Legion in a paper's home city are examples of this kind of thing. Temporary departments could be introduced to help the busy reader find an organized account of these events. Nevertheless, if there is merit in the idea of departmentalized news, this tendency toward shifting department headings should be resisted. It resembles too much the orthodox page-one philosophy of news display, which throws all kinds of news helter skelter at the reader.

Setting up regular but specialized departments like science or aviation would in effect dismember the present categories of general news—local, telegraph, and cable. These categories would be reserved for the weightier matters such as politics, economics, and social or civic affairs which form the framework of our national and municipal life. If these more ponderous departments were edited with a strong accent on condensation, background, and interpretation there would be little danger of making them dull, of losing that element of freshness and surprise (and confusion) which the reader now gets on finding "Johnson Joins Ranks of Court Plan Foes" and "Rob Women of Party Gems" side by side.

Separating the politico-economic material from that in more specialized departments, moreover, would do more than merely organize and simplify the news for the reader. For if new departments devoted to medicine, to law, to marriages and divorces, to the human-interest sideshow, to pets and what not were set up, the editorial staff would be challenged to dig up interesting facts to print in them. The reader in Massachusetts, for example, would be more interested in a medical discovery or legal dictum that affects his own life, even though news of it is taken from the pages of a medical or legal journal, than in a wire story telling him that thirteen men have been entombed in a Colorado mine.

Splitting up the daily budget of general news would not only make events easier for the reader to grasp, but it would stimulate the discovery and reporting of interesting items now overlooked.

III

In appearance, also, the inside pages of the departmentalized newspaper ought to be brighter than the average standard paper of today. Just as a store window display as a whole is more effective than the sum of its parts, so a departmentalized newspaper skillfully put together ought to take on added life and interest. The typographical formula of the news magazines could hardly be used as a model, for to spread classified department running heads and brief, magazine-type headlines over a newspaper page, even with liberal use of cuts, might lead to a vast gray acreage of reading matter.

Clearly visible and typographically snappy department running heads, to be sure, would have to be used. For most departments there would have to be on hand a full supply of them in widths all the way from single-column to full-page measure. Then the classified news could be dropped into the forms quickly and conveniently, regardless of the advertising layout of the day.

Individual headlines, while more detailed and factual than those in the news weeklies, might nevertheless be simpler in a departmentalized paper than in the present standard form. For a departmentalized paper would display stories less with a desire to make them attract attention on their own account than to make them an orderly part of the news in a particular field of human affairs. Thus in a departmentalized paper there is even greater justification than usual for simplified top heads and the smaller stories might be displayed with flexible one-column heads like those discussed in Chapter V—heads which might consist of a single word, or of half a dozen or more words in two or even three lines, set flush at left. With a head like this, a story could be dropped into the forms wherever there was space available, and the same head could stand at the top of a column and down at the bottom if the story were demoted in a later edition.

IV

Typographically, then, classification presents no insuperable difficulties. But what about the mechanics of copy-reading and the like? Although a metropolitan paper has yet to try it, there is reason to believe that the office routine involved might be simpler, if anything, than the make-up systems now in use. Certainly that is the testimony of the two small Florida papers now classifying the news—The Palm Beach Times and The Daytona Beach Morning Journal. This, too, is the experience of The Richmond Times-Dispatch, the first medium-sized paper to adopt departmentalization.

Just what office routine would be set up depends on the extent of the departure from the desk systems of today. If a paper were to go in for more background and interpretation than now, it would have rewrite desks of experts for each of its major news categories. These could also be charged with making up their own departments. At the opposite end of the scale, a paper that kept its news methods exactly what they are now but wanted to classify its news would merely have to slug each story for the proper department as it left the desk. With the simple headline schedule permissible in departmentalized pages and with no front-page display problem, there would be less of a tendency to hold a story for determination of the size of its head, and there would be less rewriting and resetting of heads in different sizes. When make-up time came, the stories would be already grouped by departments in the composing room galleys. Then they would be made up much as now in the spaces alloted previously in accordince with the advertising schedule for the day.

In sum, it does not seem more difficult to offer the reader his news in orderly fashion than it is to throw at him a mass of facts, all interesting or important, but unrelated. The world itself is interesting, but too complicated to be taken in at one gulp: "Court Orders End of Sit-Down Strike—Trader's Wife Indicted, Murder Charged on Basis of Gun Gift Clue—Child Labor Act Wins at Albany—Cairo Periled Anew as Ohio River Rises—Helena Shaken by New Tremor—Tire Workers Oust Goodyear Official—Jean Harlow Ill with Flu on Train—Wide Building Strike Averted as 42 Sign Up—King Leopold Plays Bridge with Gustav—Paid $19,000 in Cafe Racket, Two Testify—23 Soldiers Die in Alps Snowslide" . . . to quote from one paper's recent front-page assortment. Why not help the reader see this confusing world in orderly perspective?

Some Testimony about Departmentalized News

I

As MOST NEWSPAPER MEN KNOW, two small Florida dailies switched from the standard American form of news display in the fall of 1936 and began completely departmentalizing their news. Although the problems on these papers differ from those of metropolitan dailies, their experience is interesting. Don Morris, general manager of The Palm Beach Post and Times, reports on his experiment as follows:

During the late spring and early summer of 1936, after the season had eased off sufficiently to allow us to think a little about fishing and also about methods of improving our newspapers, we at The Post-Times cast about for means of giving readers better papers.

Already we had noted the method used by The Washington Star of presenting what we call a background precede in connection with certain stories. . . . We watched the use of this background precede with interest, although not making any move at the time to adopt it. Subsequently, while reading some of the weekly news magazines, I realized with something of a shock that I was getting more real information on national and foreign affairs from them than I was from our own newspapers. This was something that seemed to call for immediate correction. . . .

Slowly—very slowly indeed—the idea of a completely departmentalized newspaper, presenting also interpretation and background with the necessary stories was developed. The idea seemed so good, and yet it was so radical that we were afraid to step into it suddenly lest the water be too cold. Consequently we decided to publish a sample paper, using the type already standing from a regular edition. On Saturday, August 15, 1936, we did this. . . .

We started [regular] publication on September 21 of the afternoon Times as a completely departmentalized newspaper—the first in America. On that day and the following one we used a little extra help in the mechanical staff to make sure we would not get into trouble. Since then the new style has not cost us an extra nickel in any department. We have overcome make-up problems very simply by using combination men instead of straight make-up men. Obviously, make-up must be a little later than it is on the ordinary paper, but our plan prevents the need for extra help.

In the news room copy is handled more easily because it is not necessary to hold up any stories to determine length and page position or size of head. They all go down as they come in, slugged for their proper department, and when sufficient type is available to close a department, it is automatically closed; and anything hot breaking in that department thereafter is placed on page one under an unclassified heading of "Late News Flashes." To maintain the newspaper's show window, page one, we use banner heads which have tag lines showing which department the story may be found in, and on which page. The copy desk has been instructed that these banner lines may be used all the way down to the fold, if necessary. This system gives even more newsstand display than we previously had. . . .

At the beginning of the experiment the two most prominent criticisms from other newspaper men concerned advertising position and make-up difficulties. I have already described how we handle make-up satisfactorily, and I am happy to say that to date we have not found one advertiser who objects to the new style or demands special position because of it.

So I say we are satisfied, and—more important—our readers are too.

II

On October 1, 1936, The Daytona Beach News-Journal revived its morning edition, after a lapse of nine years, in departmentalized form. Herbert M. Davidson, editor, has this to say of his experiences:

Internally, the new system works like a charm. It is God's gift to the copyreader and also to the composing room. Each piece of copy carries two slugs, one with the name of the department, the other with the one-line head which is later to be set in 12-point italics. Three proofs are pulled. Two go to the proof-reader, one to be filed and one to be proof-read. The third proof goes to the news editor who uses it in the last hour or so before press time to write the 16 streamer heads which fill the double purpose of a news index and of newsstand attraction. The news editor also makes a copy of the captions which go immediately over the stories. This copy goes direct to the 12-point machine and these captions are set up if not all at once at least in generous takes as the evening progresses. Meanwhile, the news editor keeps a record of the number of items sent out for each classification and the number of inches required for each classification. These things make make-up very easy and rapid.

Similar systems are employed by the sports editor and the society editor. I believe we are the only newspaper which has carried departmentalization into these fields as well as utilizing it for straight news.

What we have done here is really only the first step toward a fundamental change which I believe is inevitable in morning newspapers. Until now morning papers, for no particular reason other than that which causes sheep to follow a herd, have been mere imitations both in content and in style of afternoon newspapers, which as the processes of news transmission and newspaper manufacture have speeded up have at least in middle-sized cities walked away with both circulation and advertising. Add to other influences the fact that the radio as a disseminator of news is most effective in the evening and you can readily realize how ineffective the morning paper is becoming as a conveyor of spot or bulletin news. In other words, there is less spot news than ever available first to morning papers, and a part of this already has been divulged to families sitting at home listening to radios.

As I see it the problems of a morning paper must become more and more those of the organizer and interpreter of news, or to put it in one word, the review. The work of the weekly news journals must be speeded up into a daily process and become the field of the morning newspaper.

Now I would not be so absurd as to suggest that this has been accomplished by a mere typographical arrangement . . . [like that of The Morning Journal]. But that is as far as I can go with a small newspaper in a small city operating largely with moderately-paid assistants and consequently under the need of avoiding overset and other excessive expenditures.

The possibilities in a larger city are so tremendous that they make me bite my lips with impatience because I am not privileged to try them out. I am referring particularly to the opportunities of remodeling the content of the paper to fit a departmentalized typography.

III

The largest American newspaper which at the time of writing has departmentalized its news is The Richmond Times-Dispatch in Virginia. Shortly after the change was made on March 30, 1937, Leon S. Dure, Jr., executive editor, said:

I have been interested in the idea for two or three years, and at one time we planned to put it into effect last year. As it happened, however, the then publisher, Mark Ethridge, left Richmond for Louisville, and it was necessarily delayed. I might add that John D. Wise, the present publisher, is just as enthusiastic about the idea as was Mark Ethridge. . . .

When we began our present system last week, I had little fear of the reader reaction to the new paper, but I must confess an anxiety as to the advertisers. Our advertising manager, and most of the others in the business office, were dead against it. You can image, therefore, how I felt—how we all feel—when the reaction everywhere was overwhelmingly favorable, and even enthusiastic. It is obvious that the reader interest inside of the Times-Dispatch is from twenty to fifty per cent greater than it was before. And we always were a careful, well-organized paper.

In an office memorandum distributed to the staff before the change went into effect, Mr. Dure wrote:

The whole idea is based on the belief that the newspaper today somehow lacks the horsepower it once had, and that this is true because old formulas for handling news are no longer adequate. We believe that a growing number of newspaper men are coming to the same conclusion, that what is needed is a thoroughgoing overhauling of the whole news structure.

To begin with, the influence of radio and the newsreels is undeniable. Gone is the thrill of a Bangkok dateline when the reader has only to turn a dial to hear the late King of England in a very personal conversation. The reader, like the quail, has been getting harder and harder to creep upon and startle.

Granting this, and granting further that the reader is becoming more and more demanding of the facts behind the facts, we believe that the answer quite frankly is to be found in the magazine Time. . . . We do not mean by that that we propose to ape Time in the matter of style. What might appear in fairly good grace in a national magazine might well, and probably would, violate good taste in the home-town journal. What we propose to do, simply is to present new facts in an orderly manner, reinforced by the old facts that give them perspective.

To do this it is necessary to segregate news into departments. Where we now have sports and women's departments, we will in future also have departments for national affairs, science, religion, and the dozen or more other logical news classifications. These departments will be operated by a group of copy editors, growing out of the present copy desk.

As we see it, the argument is all in favor of news classification. Under present methods, the reader of foreign affairs finishes a piece on Mussolini to be informed that the Ladies' Aid Society of the First Baptist Church is planning another rummage sale, or that a new dust storm is forming in the West. The harassed business man has to scan every item in the paper to make sure that he hasn't missed something of business significance.

We believe that when the reader comes to the end of one story dealing with conditions abroad he is psychologically set up for more of the same mental fare. We believe, furthermore, that when two related stories are put together the sum of the whole, in reader interest, is greater than the sum of the two stories apart.

To turn the argument around, no one but a fool would suggest that we break up the sports pages and print one sports story on every page in the paper. Yet that is exactly what newspapers have been doing with other categories of news. The value of segregation is strikingly shown by the growth of sports interest that accompanied this segregation. . . .

Classification of news also will cure many of the ills of the present system. Stories can be written shorter and more to the point. A definite check can be established on every situation so that stories will be followed up. Background material can be inserted from day to day to give real meaning to continuing stories without being tiresome. . . .

The paths ahead are uncharted but the main emphasis will be on the news story—to make it interesting and to make it understandable.

When the subject of departmentalization is brought up among newspaper men, almost inevitably some unconvinced editor will object that it is mechanically impossible. If all news is departmentalized, all pages will be held open until the last moment. How then can one escape a bottleneck in the stereotyping department? Questioned on this point, Mr. Dure replied:

You ask me about how we prevent stereotyping jams, caused by releasing pages all together. We are now constructing new make-up tables, provided with vertical racks in which we store departmentalized time copy—and by time copy I do not mean trivia, but decent stories and features culled from magazines and other sources. When a department runs short it is a simple matter to adjust the page by using this material.

Our experience so far has been just this: it was always hard to make an 11:40 deadline; and it is now hard to make an 11:40 deadline, but the troubles under the new system are no greater than they were before.

IV

Following is a list of possible newspaper departments for a completely classified newspaper. It was prepared by synthesizing the departments used by the three present departmentalized papers, The Palm Beach Times, The Daytona Beach Morning Journal, and The Richmond Times-Dispatch, together with those in Time, News-Week, Literary Digest, and Pathfinder. It omits only specialized non-news classifications like humor, comics, and fiction, and some detailed material found in metropolitan papers like shipping and mails, Army, Navy, and police orders, or arrival of buyers.

This list is presented as a workable maximum which might be simplified to meet the needs of any individual newspaper:

Page One.—This can be either a front page of leading departments, as in the two Florida departmentalized papers; unclassified, as in the Times-Dispatch; or a page devoted to summaries of all the news throughout the paper. A possible page-one subdivision for afternoon papers is *Late News Flashes.*

Local News.—Anything happening in the city or environs which does not belong in specialized departments like *Law, Medicine, Finance,* or *Sports.*

State News.—Legislative, political, and general telegraph news from outside the city suburbs and inside the state boundaries.

National Affairs.—Political and general telegraph news. The two may be separated into *Politics* and *National News.* Washington gossip columns and related material might again be segregated.

Labor.—This department would draw material now being printed as national or local news, and which in the early part of 1937 has been one of the big continuing stories. Displaying this news separately might, as in other departments, lead to more thorough coverage than is usual when there is no big strike under way.

Foreign Affairs.—Any cable news, or Washington news tied up with foreign news, belongs here.

Crime.—A convenient running head in which comparable items from all over the country, and indeed the world, can be displayed together. A major local robbery or national kidnapping belongs here rather than with local or national news.

Disasters and Accidents.—Same as Crime, but for a different group of stories.

Business and Finance.—All industrial, commercial, banking and money news that does not, like the steel strike, belong with *National News* because of its social or political importance. Further subdivisions might be *Advertising* and *Real Estate.*

Markets.—The usual financial tables plus comment and news directly concerned with them.

Transportation.—A catch-all for news of shipping, railroads, buses, automobiles, trailers, and air transport. It might be further subdivided into separate categories like the late Literary Digest's *Wheels, Ships,* and *Wings.*

Miscellany.—This is a department appearing in all departmentalized publications under names such as *Features, Side-show, Off-Side, Americana, The Human Side,* and *Parade.* It includes news oddities, human interest stories, and those items of semi-feature news which by nature will not fit into other categories. The Richmond Times-Dispatch has a separate department headed *Animals.*

Headliners (also called variously *Names, Names That Make*

News, Presenting, and *People*).—Brief sketches of new persons in the news or items about well-known persons.

Sports.—Like business and financial news this category of news is pretty well departmentalized now. Readers might find their way about still more easily, however, if the various sports were presented under running heads identifying whatever was going on: Baseball, Hockey, Racing, Badminton, Skiing. Then the hockey fan will not risk wasting his time by reading the boxing item "Barlund to Meet Berman on Jan. 20" printed just below the story reporting that Chabot will replace Worters as goal for the New York Americans.

Entertainment or *Amusements.*—Here again a catch-all department might be run or, better, *Theater, Screen, Radio, Books, Music,* and *Art* might each have a department head for the benefit of the reader who is looking for news or views about any one of them.

Agriculture.—A must with any newspaper serving a farming area, or a business center dependent on farming. In industrial cities agricultural news might belong more properly in the *National Affairs* and *Business* groupings.

Science.—A similar general category, much better divided when the news warrants into *Science* proper plus *Medicine* (and public health) and perhaps *Aviation.* Now that the latter has emerged from the freak and inventive stage it belongs more properly, however, with the *Transportation* group of departments.

Religion.—This department might be devoted not only to Saturday and Monday church news but also to general (and perhaps more interesting to a lay audience) news indicated by the newsweekly department heads *Religion and Society,* and *Social Service.*

Education.—Not only local news about schools but also general and feature news of interest to parents and educators. The ousting of Glenn Frank from the University of Wisconsin belongs here.

The Press.—Here the news weeklies have done a better job than the papers, which neglect news of their own affairs unless a Captain Patterson signs with the Guild or some important newspaper is sold.

Law.—Suited chiefly to metropolitan papers, but one place where much could be done.

Travel.—When there is news of this kind which interests the reader as well as the advertising department, it might be brought out of the Sunday sections and given a department head of its own in the daily pages. Ship news in maritime cities might go with it. Or it might form part of the *Transportation* department.

Letters.—The one clearly identified and labelled department which every American newspaper runs already.

Women's Page.—Again a customary department, to which are related *Society News, Food Market* and *Household News, Recipes,* and *Women's Clubs.*

Personal.—News of divorces, engagements, marriages, births, and deaths belong here. The Palm Beach Times records births and obituaries together under *Vital Statistics.* The news weeklies, under heads like *Transition* and *Milestones,* record in these departments also illnesses of prominent persons, awards made to them, and comparable personal items.

Weather.—Again a department common to all American dailies, though one might wish for more frequent translation of meteorological jargon into English.

Writing the News

I

PIERRE DENOYER, AMERICAN CORRESPONDENT of Le Petit Parisien, lectured not long ago at the Graduate School of Journalism at Columbia University. "When an American [newspaper man] writes his story," he said, "he has to repeat, taking each individual part of the lead and giving a more complete version of what is summarized in the lead. This repetition is irritating to a French reader." It is also irritating, one might add, to an American reader.

The reason for this repetition, Mr. Denoyer added, is the practicality of the inverted-pyramid, or standard American form, of news story. The essence of all the news is told immediately at the beginning, so that the reader at once knows what the story is about and can decide whether he wants to read it or not. The details are developed in the body of the story, which finally trails off into minor paragraphs in the end. These last paragraphs the make-up man can lift out if necessary in order to make the type fit forms in the hurry of closing an edition, and they will hardly be missed.

Perhaps this formula has become more important than the end originally sought. At least one wonders whether its advantages in practice justify its sometimes strange results in news writing. Something like this has impressed itself upon another Frenchman, Raoul de Roussy de Sales, American correspondent of Paris-Soir, who wrote in the January, 1937, Atlantic Monthly:

Let us suppose that one of the dictators—and I don't care which—is murdered tomorrow. This, in France, will probably be front-page stuff, in spite of Louis VI, and the story will run something like this: "It was one of these exquisite autumn days. The sun was sinking slowly behind the purple mountains. Its last rays were caressing (ses derniers rayons caressaient) the shining helmets of the mounted guards surrounding the car of the man who for so many years has been the idol of his countrymen. No one could imagine that this man, who, at that moment, was smiling and bowing to an ecstatic crowd, would in a very few seconds take his place in the Elysian Fields. But human destiny, etc. . . . History has been made and undone many times in such a way, and, as Pascal said apropos of Cleopatra's nose, etc. . . . Suddenly a shot was heard. A man whose eyes were shining like those of a panther. . . ."

In other words, the French newspaper writer will lead you up dramatically to the climax in such a way that when you get there your pulse will be up around 120.

His American confrere, on the other hand, will knock you out cold in the first paragraph, thus: "Dictator Blank was fatally shot at 5:16 P.M. by an assassin while driving through the main thoroughfare of Zed. His assailant, who gave his name as Enrico Levinsky, 213 Brutus Avenue, was taken into custody by the police."

From then on the story will have a tendency to repeat itself with slight variations, incidental details being added here and there as the columns unwind, like a string of sausages. This method of mechanical amplification has obvious advantages, especially for the editor. With a pair of scissors he can cut the story at any point, because, provided he leaves the headlines and the first paragraph, everything worth knowing will be there.

The French reporter *tells* a story; the American *covers* it. One must choose the details and present them in such a way that a definite impression will be created; the other is asked to collect the greatest possible number of facts as if he were assembling the material for an article in an encyclopaedia. Both methods have their advantages and their inconveniences, but I will venture to say that the American system produces an impression of dullness which is sometimes very disheartening.

Let us analyze a specific story, selecting as an example one published in The New York Times in the fall of 1936. This story, which occupied twenty-one inches of type without its headline, began thus:

WILLIAMSTOWN, MASS., Oct. 12.—The Mark Hopkins Centenary at Williams College ended today with a colorful academic procession, the award of nine honorary degrees and an address by President Tyler Dennett in which he announced bequests totaling $2,400,000 from Samuel Hopkins, New York cotton merchant and cousin of Mark Hopkins, who died in New York City in June.

This lead, it will be noted, contains among other things a reference to the academic procession, to the award of honorary degrees, to President Dennett's address, and to the bequests to the college. The writer then went on, as Mr. Denoyer says, "taking each individual part of the lead and giving a more complete version" of it. If we identify each of the succeeding paragraphs of this story by a key word (address, bequests, and so forth) and give it a number indicating how many times that particular item has been referred to, the whole takes the following pattern:

Lead:
Procession (1); degrees (1); address (1); bequests (1).
Succeeding paragraphs:
Bequests (2); bequests (3); address (2); address (3); degrees (2); degrees (3); luncheon (1) [a detail not given in the lead]; luncheon (2); procession (2); address (4) [followed by 8 more paragraphs on the same subject]; bequests (3); bequests (4).

After the lead, then, this story jumps to bequests, to the president's address again, to honorary degrees a second time, to the luncheon, back to the procession again, then to the address once more for full details, and finally to the bequests for the third and last time.

This story was run under the by-line of William L. Laurence, 1937 Pulitzer Prize co-winner for his stories on the Harvard Tercentenary, and long known as one of the distinguished science writers of the country. That fact plus the certainty that the newspaper publishing his story is in the forefront of the world's journalism should be sufficient indication that the story's repetition and the resulting irritation to the reader come not from lack of skill, but from something else. It comes from observance of the standard American formula for writing news.

Most of us have encountered this kind of thing in our daily consumption of newsprint so often that it is all too familiar. Another example, however, may be useful because it reveals a different manifestation of the same thing. The New York Times, again, displayed on its front page of March 18, 1936, a story headed: "Germans Accept the League's Bid; British Pave Way." A crossline in the head added: "Delegates Arrive Today." Then, after the succeeding banks in the head came three news summaries outlining three stories dealing with this event. The London summary said: "Her [Germany's] delegates will sit at a session today," and the Berlin summary repeated, *"A delegation of twenty will fly to London headed by Joachim von Ribbentrop."* Then followed the London story itself, which began *"A German delegation headed by Joachim von Ribbentrop . . ."* and took the rest of the column before being jumped to a lengthy continuation on page 12. In this continuation was the text of a telegram from Baron von Neurath, German Foreign Minister, to the British Foreign Office, saying once again that the delegation was coming.

On page 13, furthermore, was the Berlin story, headed "Reich Is Sending a Big Delegation," with one of its banks telling again the now familiar story, *"Party of Twenty, Headed by von Ribbentrop, Will Fly to British Capital Today."* The story itself, one need hardly add, repeated in the lead the news that *"The delegation that will represent Germany . . . will comprise Joachim von Ribbentrop . . . It will fly to London tomorrow morning."* Well down in the body of the story we are told that *"The chief if not exclusive function of Mr. von Ribbentrop, who heads the German delegation"* is so and so. And then, to make sure the reader gets the news, this story is followed by an A.P. item under a tiny subhead saying, *"Party Will Number Twenty."* This item begins, after a Berlin dateline, *"Two special airplanes will depart tomorrow bearing a German delegation to the London meeting . . . The Germans will arrive in England about twenty strong."*

That morning's Times, in sum, told us no less than eleven different times the fact, in whole or in part, that a German delegation of twenty, headed by Joachim von Ribbentrop, was flying to London. Why not say it once in the head and once in the story—and let it go at that?

Lest anyone imagine that the Times is alone in thus repeating its news, consider this A.P. item sent over the wires on March 4, 1936:

LONDON, March 4 (A.P.).—A middle-aged German lawyer-writer, accused of espionage upon Great Britain's air force, heard documents read in Old Bailey Court today tending to implicate him in spying on American air forces during the World War.

The trial, Great Britain's first one for espionage since the war, saw the defendant, Dr. Hermann Gortz, blink when he heard his own description of himself as a *"dangerous intelligence officer"* turned against him.

The Crown presented a document Dr. Gortz had written to the German Government describing his intelligence work during the World War and mentioning that he lived for a year and a half in the United States and three and a half years in London.

During that period, the letter said, he was "again in contact with American and British wartime aviators" and *"I am even now still in touch with military aviators on the active list, or I probably can get in touch with them again."*

The Crown said Dr. Gortz applied in 1935 to the German Air Ministry for a job as a spy but was refused.

One document quoted Dr. Gortz as saying of his World War service: "On two American air force officers who were shot down was found a warning referring to me as a *particularly dangerous intelligence officer* and containing an exact personal description of me."

The statement said while Dr. Gortz was in New York and Chicago in 1925 and 1926 he met American air force officers whom he had questioned during the war and was introduced to aviation clubs and war veterans' organizations. He was forced to leave America, it was said, because he refused to become a citizen.

"I am even now still in touch with military aviators on the active list, or I probably can get in touch with them again," said the document.

Two women are on the jury trying Dr. Gortz. . . .

Setting the repetition in italics, or lifting it out as in the previous examples, may make these stories appear more ludicrous than they really are. Yet any reader who is not knocked between the eyes by such repetition must have a mind all calloused by frequent rubbing against the inverted-pyramid form of news story. Is it any wonder that Mr. Denoyer finds the practice irritating and that Mr. de Roussy de Sales gets from it an impression of dullness which is sometimes disheartening?

II

If there is a case against the American news story on the ground of repetition, there is also another on the ground of unnecessary length. And for an example of crisp news writing I can do no better than to quote the following from The Japan Advertiser in Tokyo. The story was evidently rewritten from a dispatch sent out by Rengo, the Japanese news agency:

DYNAMITE UNITES LOVERS

Unhappy Couple Embrace, Light Fuse to End Troubles

Jisaku Yaguchi, 37, stone worker of Shiraku-mura, Kasagun, Kyoto Prefecture, fell in love with Yoshiko Shibuya, 34, housekeeper at a local inn. But he had a wife and five children, so they couldn't get married. Yesterday morning the two went to a hut on Onami beach on the outskirts of Shin Maizuru-machi, embraced, placed a stick of dynamite between them and lit the fuse. The result was gruesome, said Rengo.

What more need be said? Yet the average American paper would have told this tale in at least twice and perhaps four times the space, while our supposedly condensed tabloids—since the result was gruesome—could be relied upon to play it even longer than that. They might also have added the personal signed story of Jisaku's unhappy relict. And certainly all American papers would have used the far less dramatic inverted-pyramid form.

It is not alone in police or human-interest stories that condensation can be practiced to advantage. When delegates from the United States, Great Britain, and Japan met in London in the closing months of 1934 to discover whether it was worth while to hold a formal naval conference in 1935, the American press devoted daily columns to the event. But Time magazine reported one whole week of these talks as follows:

DAVIS TWO UP

At the deadlocked London naval parley between Britain, the U.S., and Japan (Time, Oct. 29), U. S. Ambassador Norman Hezekiah Davis last week worsted Japanese Ambassador Tsuneo Matsudaira two up at golf. There was no other progress. Said inflexible Japanese Chief Delegate Rear Admiral Isoroku Yamamoto, broadcasting around the world to the Japanese people, "I am in no hurry. I will do my best to attain the Government's objectives and live up to Japan's expectations." These expectations: Britain and the U.S. shall accord Japan naval parity, scrapping the 5-5-3 ratio.

It need hardly be said that a national weekly can compress this kind of thing more readily than a metropolitan daily. A newspaper must give daily spot news coverage of such a vital item in the world's procession of events. But must it take so much space for it?

In the belief that far more condensation than usual is possible, some experimental work along these lines was done recently at the Graduate School of Journalism at Columbia (see illustration, page 99). Two dummy pages containing the results of this and other experiments were prepared, using The New York Herald Tribune of March 3, 1937—a date chosen at random—as raw material to be reworked. This was the issue containing the news that the Carnegie-Illinois Steel Corporation, chief producing unit of U. S. Steel, had signed a collective bargaining agreement recognizing the Committee for Industrial Organization. On the same day appeared related stories—the President's coming out in support of new wage-and-hour legislation replacing N.R.A., the report of the President's post-mortem committee on N.R.A., the fact that the steel agreement presaged the end of the Navy Department's difficulties under the Walsh-Healey Act, two more sit-down strikes in Detroit, and numerous items of strike news, great and small.

In the Herald Tribune these events took half the front page

plus parts of pages 10, 11, and 12. Pictures, heads, and text totaled more than 210 column inches in all. In the experimental pages—a front page devoted entirely to news summaries plus a sample departmentalized inside page—the identical news was told in 119 inches. The experimental pages used far larger type—9-on-10 point —but wider columns made the word-count approximately equal, so that the comparison is fair. And the general reader comparing the two versions of the same news will find, I think, that nothing has been omitted from the condensed version. In a few places, indeed, added background or interpretive material has been worked in. The saving was accomplished on the inside news page simply by telling each subordinate part of each news story adequately, but once and once only.

In fairness it must be admitted that the dummy pages were prepared at leisure, with no problem of meeting an edition deadline—in other words, with plenty of time available for rewrite. Yet the fact remains that condensation from the accepted forms of today is possible, and I think desirable.

American papers are read eagerly, but by no means thoroughly. The Gallup surveys indicate that, on a rough average, only 10 percent of a metropolitan newspaper is read. The straight-news sections show up a little better than this average, and obviously even here many more stories than a given subscriber will read must be printed. But must they be as long as they are?

III

Speaking of these and similar matters recently Floyd M. Felmly, managing editor of The Newark Evening News, told of an experience with an unusually complicated spot news story. There had been in Newark a robbery involving murder, followed by an intricate train of events which involved escape, accidental pursuit, more shootings, and final capture of the criminals. The reporter assigned to the story, faced with so tangled a web of events, was stumped when it came to casting them into the pattern of the inverted-pyramid story. With the deadline approaching, he took his problem to Mr. Felmly, who said: "Why don't you write a simple, comprehensive lead saying what it is all about, and then get right into a chronological story, beginning at the beginning and following through to the end, just the way it happened."

The reporter did just that, and turned in a story that won praise both inside and outside the office. It was a good story. Why? Is there not a clue here that might lead to cleaner and fresher copy than we often get in our newspapers?

The formula followed by Fortune magazine when it seeks to tell about some vast corporate enterprise is to the point. A beginning is made somewhere. Usually there is not even a comprehensive lead, since the problem of a magazine in presenting an article is obviously different from that of a newspaper. Each part of the whole is then taken up in its place. In single file the various elements are told briefly or at length as may be needed, but they are told once only. The finished article gives a surprisingly clear story to the reader, with the various parts taking their place in a well-ordered perspective. There is not the constant weaving back and forth, the telling and retelling of facts and their relationships, which so often marks the attempt to distort the event as it was when it happened into the shape of an inverted-pyramid. And if the headline continues its function of giving the meat of the news, what is lost? Certainly nothing the reader would miss, and much in the way of repetition and length he would gladly do without.

Perhaps the make-up man would be troubled if he had to use each story as a whole or not at all, without the possibility of lifting out those conveniently unimportant last paragraphs. But how often does he really do that now? Does he not at least as often fit the type into the forms simply by using those stories which pretty closely fit the space and omitting those less important ones which do not fit? It would seem that he could stick to this method exclusively and get along with no more of a crisis over each page than he has now.

In the belief that this could be done the experimental pages referred to earlier in this chapter were written according to this chronological, or at least logical, formula for writing news. The leading story for the day told of United States Steel's recognition of C.I.O. In the Herald Tribune, which served as guinea pig in the experiment, it was an excellent piece of A.P. wire copy from Pittsburgh written in the standard form. This story, taking thirty inches of body type, led off with the high spot—formal recognition of organized labor by Big Steel. Then came news of the contract signed, which established the forty-hour week and a $5-a-day minimum and provided for a more detailed agreement later. Then, right in the body of the story, followed the full text of the agreement, which of course repeated much of the information already given in outline form. There followed comment from Philip Murray, the labor organizer who had signed the agreement, a paragraph on the stock market reaction, and another lifting out a significant point in Mr. Murray's statement. At this point the story was jumped to page ten, and inside came details of the conference which was to negotiate the detailed agreement and a statement from the company repeating news of the forty-hour week and giving some new details. Next was an account of other steel companies which had taken similar action, the previous activities of the labor organizers, and a bit of background. Then more news of what had preceded the agreement, and at the end a statement of when and how the whole movement to organize the industry had begun. On page one was a brief separate statement from John L. Lewis, and on page ten, the jump page, another separate story giving the opinion of New York steel men on the news and some statistics about the industry.

The experimentally-rewritten version of this story takes less than twenty inches of body type, even though it includes the news of all three of the original items, which totaled forty inches in the Herald Tribune. It includes also some background material which did not appear in the original at all. Because in the experimental version the essence of the news is given in headline and summary on page one, the story itself is displayed on page two, all in one place, under a simple two-column head saying "Steel Signs C.I.O. Contract, Reversing Historic Labor Policy." This story is divided into three parts, marked off by large and easily-visible subheads. The first part, under the subhead "The Setting," begins at the beginning by giving background and explaining events leading up to the spot news. (The usual spot-news lead could be omitted because of the front-page material and the head over this inside story.) The second part, headed "What Happened," tells just that, in chronological order. The third, "Results," notes the effects in the industry, gives Wall Street's reaction, and tells the opinion of New York steel men about the news.

One of the greatest economies in reducing this material from forty to twenty inches was in using the text of the agreement between Carnegie-Steel and C.I.O. In 1918 The New York Times won the Pulitzer Prize for public service because of its innovation, developed during the World War, of printing the full text of official reports, documents, and speeches. In a time when governments everywhere sought to conceal facts with all sorts of false fronts, this service was invaluable. In today's confused and confusing world this practice, now followed by other newspapers, remains an indispensable part of the mechanism of distributing information. The newspaper of record, let us hope, is here to stay. At the same time one may ask how many subscribers read these priceless full texts.

The many who do not bother with the full text are expected to read the accompanying news story, where the text is paraphrased for them. But so far as the overwhelming majority of readers is concerned, does not this method waste space? Is it necessary to say in the headlines and again in the lead that such-and-such a text was signed or published, then to give some of the details in succeeding paragraphs, and perhaps to give some of them in still greater detail farther on—and then to print the entire text separately as well? For professors, officials, some business men, and other interested individuals the entire text is essential. But whether it is essential for all newspaper readers is a question.

It seems to me that there is room here for an editorial function which in its field could be as useful as that of the newspaper of record in its own. A newspaper designed for the general reader might scrupulously and painstakingly pick over the full text for its essential parts, and print these in quotes, with the extensive elisions and omissions clearly indicated. No retelling of the story as a separate news story would then be necessary. The reader would be given access to the news itself in a form which would attract rather than discourage its reading. The newspaper would do a better job in less space.

IV

In order to attain the perfection of simplicity and directness sought in the earlier sections of this chapter, two further steps might be necessary: the writing of all background or other outside elements of the news directly into the story in its proper place without brackets, three-em dashes, bold-face, or other typographical impedimenta; and the exclusion of datelines, by-lines, self-glorification in the way of boasts about exclusive news, or any other trivia which get between the reader and the news itself.

A year ago Editor & Publisher said in an editorial:

Without sacrifice of a line of worthwhile press association copy or a syndicate feature that is worth its present space, newspapers can go new places with their readers by editing that is not mere mechanical reading and head-writing, and a guard against errors and libel, but critical, constructive elaboration of ideas that readers must comprehend more than dimly for the welfare of one and all.

Indeed it is no longer necessary to argue, I think, that background and interpretation are vital adjuncts of the news. Even two years ago (when Chapter I was first published in the Atlantic Monthly) this was something of a heresy. And grave doubt still exists in the minds of all but a few editors as to whether background material can be displayed as an integral part of, rather than as an addition to, the news. Yet nowadays one finds the material itself in the American newspaper so often that one wonders whether this is not a question of typography rather than one of ethics.

I have before me, for example, the leading story in The New

York World Telegram of September 24, 1936. It is Lester Ziffren's cable from Madrid to the United Press telling of a flood which temporarily stopped the rebel advance on Toledo. The story runs down the page two columns wide, but after the first two paragraphs it is interrupted by the following item, set exactly like the rest except that it is in slightly narrower measure and in brackets:

[Information was still too meager to judge the full effects of the flood, but unless government announcements are exaggerated the rebels appear to have been checkmated effectively for the time being in the west. The Teuan (Morocco) rebel radio reported late today that a rebel column had arrived in the outskirts of Toledo and engaged in violent combat with government forces at the gates of the city. The report was not confirmed by other sources.]

The main story then runs on for two more brief paragraphs, to be followed by another indented one in brackets:

[Earlier United Press dispatches from Madrid today reported the rebel offensive on Toledo had been stopped, but the correspondent, telephoning to London with a censor listening in, was unable to state specifically at that time why. That the halt might have been only temporary was indicated in an Associated Press dispatch from insurgent forces at Torrijos saying that after a brief rest the rebels had resumed their advance toward Toledo.]

If these paragraphs had been written into the story exactly as they were, but not differentiated typographically from the rest, the going would have been a little less jerky for the reader, and every propriety of objectivity and credit to another press association would have been met.

It stands to reason that a newspaper office can gather a more complete account of a big story from all sources than can a single reporter at one news center. Why not bring these separate threads of information all together, no matter what their source, credit them so far as needed, and weave them into a single smooth-flowing unit that makes things easy for the reader? What useful purpose do the brackets and indentations serve? Or why is it better to print a cable item intact, as many papers do, and then follow it under a three-em dash with a shirt-tail or dash-matter of explanation, instead of rewriting the whole as a comprehensive unit, with each fact told once in its proper place in the narrative?

Such a purpose might be furthered by the omission of datelines. Numerous papers have already dropped the dates. Why not drop the name of the place where the story orginates as well? Every American newspaper reports a local story by saying that "Two men were killed in a holdup of a filling station at Elm and Locust streets early this morning." Why not say "Two men were killed in a riot in Paris yesterday" as well? If the foreign story must begin with "Paris, April 1.—(I.N.S.) . . ." why must not the local story likewise begin with "Bingville Police Headquarters, April 1.— (Special to the Bugle) . . .?" The necessary press association credit in stories, now run under a dateline, could do just as well at the end of the story as at the beginning.

To drop datelines entirely would avoid some curious inconsistencies. Characteristic of these is a New York Times story of the last presidential election campaign printed with a Washington dateline of the day before. It tells of Mr. Roosevelt's doings and of his coming speech on the evening of the day of publication. The usual boldface subhead over this part of the story says *"Tonight's* Subject Not Divulged," while the text in the very next line says, "The topic of *tomorrow night's* speech was not divulged by the White House."

Less common than the dateline habit, but still common enough to get in the way of the newspaper reader at times, is the practice of self-glorification by both correspondents and the newspapers themselves. It seems that a man cannot work abroad for long before he begins to cable home that "President Benes told your correspondent tonight that . . ." or, even worse, that the great man said it "in an exclusive interview with your correspondent." When, as sometimes happens, the home office does not give your correspondent his expected by-line, the thing is reduced to the absurd.

Exclusive stories are vital things. The effort to get them has made the newspaper the essential if unofficial part of American national and local government that it is. But one can publish exclusive stories without throwing the fact in the reader's face. For example:

By Oracle

LONDON, Oct. 15.—A direct link exists between King Leopold's historic declaration on neutrality, made yesterday, and publication in The Bingville Bugle on Aug. 12 of a message from London announcing that the Belgian Government was preparing to move toward a return to pre-war conditions.

The Bugle, by this statement, which outlined the Belgian plan exactly as it is now announced in the royal speech, created a sensation in the diplomatic corps accredited to Washington, members of which hastened to inform their government of the contents of the surprising revelation.

Since then the authorities in Brussels have been repeatedly requested from Paris and other capitals to furnish an explanation of their attitude, and every movement of Belgian diplomacy has been watched with unblinking attention.

In the fourth paragraph the story gets around to the news.

Das Ding an Sich

IN THE COURSE OF HIS METAPHYSICAL speculations the philosopher Immanuel Kant reached a conclusion which by analogy can become useful to the newspaper man. Faced with the ancient problem of how man can know the ultimate nature of reality, Kant concluded that the mind is so conditioned by time and space that it cannot know, directly, an outside object. This latter he called *das Ding an sich*—the thing in itself, as distinct from one's mental perception of it.

Without doing too great violence to Kantian epistemology, I think we can use this term to illustrate a central aspect of contemporary newspaper work. The reader, too, has difficulty in perceiving *das Ding an sich,* if we identify the latter as a news event remote from him, of which he reads; and the more complex or remote the event, the greater his difficulty. In its simpler forms this question is merely one of technique in newswriting; deeper down it becomes a question of accuracy and effectiveness in reporting.

I

So far as the technique of news writing is concerned, the problem of getting the reader in touch with *das Ding an sich,* the event of which he reads, has been aptly phrased by John Martin, managing editor of Time. "Make a picture," he tells his writers in coaching them in the ways of his publication. And I for one think that this

habit of making a picture in writing or rewriting the news deserves
credit more than condensation, research, organization of the story,
and even than those annoying quirks of phraseology which charac-
terize Time, in accounting for the spectacular success of this weekly magazine in what is in part the daily newspaper's field.

If for example the American Association of Hatbox Manufacturers, the cream of that vast and powerful industry, meets in St. Louis
to take steps to resist John L. Lewis, who is gunning for them with
C.I.O., the resultant newspaper account is likely to be something
like this:

St. Louis, April 1.—Representatives of the hatbox manufacturing
industry in the United States meeting here today adopted a resolution
stating their "unalterable opposition to the closed shop and the check-
off in the hatbox manufacturing industry." The manufacturers, among
whom are included some of the greatest names in American business,
further voted to address to President Roosevelt a memorial . . .

Time, on the other hand, would be more likely to say,

Over St. Louis last week hung a hot, breathless humidity, leaving the
air-conditioned tenth-floor ballroom of the Hotel Schmaltz an island of
comfort in a sea of sticky heat. To this ballroom hurried, from all parts
of the United States, men who . . .

Orthodox news writing, in short, tells the reader about the
news. The visual writing often used in Time, on the other hand,
transports the reader to the scene of action. Before he knows it he
himself is in the Hotel Schmaltz's convention hall, seeing, hearing,
perhaps even smelling and tasting what is going on. There is little
doubt as to which is the more readable. The ordinary American
reader is likely to find his eyes wandering as he scans the columns
which tell him that Adolf Hitler has made another sabre-rattling
speech, causing opinion in British diplomatic circles to harden,
and so forth. If, however, he is lifted out of his daily routine and
all unnoticed set down in the Olympic stadium near Berlin; if he
sees the massed thousands of uniformed Nazis standing at attention before spectacular rows of black, red, and white flags; if he

hears that vast chorus sing the Horst Wessel song, and finally
feels the thrill of the whole stupendous assemblage as The Leader
comes in, he is at the very least fascinated by the show. Something like that is made possible by writing the news itself, rather
than merely writing about it.

It need hardly be added that certain types of assignments do
not allow this kind of writing. It is a little difficult to picture the
economic results of further devaluation of the French franc in
visual terms. At the same time, could not far more use be made
of this method than now? Consider, for instance, the following
leads on two cable stories of 1935:

ROME, Oct. 20.—Faced with a formidable problem in a search for a
way to do three things at once—save Italy from a European war, give
satisfaction to Great Britain and to the League of Nations, and permit
Italy to continue with her program for Ethiopia—Premier Benito
Mussolini remained all day in meditation in his immense study in the
Palazzo Venezia while a storm lashed its windows with rain.—New
York Herald Tribune.

ROME, Oct. 20.—Persons passing the Palazzo Venezia and the Palazzo
Chigi, seats respectively of government and the Foreign Ministry, saw
them ablaze with lights up to a late hour tonight. It is obvious that the
whole staff of the Foreign Ministry is working overtime and that negotiations among London, Rome, and Paris for a solution of the Italo-
Ethiopian conflict are being actively continued.—New York Times.

Those two visual touches, rain beating on the windows and lights
blazing until late in the night, serve to help the reader see for himself the scene of action.

II

Less important, perhaps, but still helping to make the difference
between good news writing and bad, is the related matter of col-
lecting and using specific, concrete details. The good reporter will
get them; the less competent one will allow his information to
stay nearer the surface, which means that the reader is removed
by that much from the event. The ordinary writer would say, for
example, that "The President's wife holds a press conference once

a week in the White House with the women reporters assigned to her." Stanley Walker, however, put it this way: "And Mrs. Roosevelt's own conferences with the ladies of the press are informal. They are held at 11 o'clock in the morning once a week . . . on the second floor of the White House in the sitting room at the west end of the building."

Again, most feature articles on the Constitution would begin with some general statement introducing the subject, and would then take up the legal or historical considerations or whatever else was at issue. Fortune magazine, however, after its lead does not take the Constitution for granted in this fashion. It gets right down to *das Ding an sich:*

. . . Physically the Constitution of the United States is four sheets of parchment in a dustproof air-conditioned glass case on the second floor of the Library of Congress. In addition to the four sheets there are various forms and sizes of paper and parchment covered with amendments and kept under flimsy lock in a cabinet in the cellar of the State Department.

Touches like that are bound to make the reader feel that he is in contact with the thing of which he reads; not only will it serve him by facilitating his grasp of the subject matter, but it will make him enjoy his reading the more.

Most news stories are narratives, narratives of action, and action stories appeal to the lowest common denominator in the masses who make up the reading public. Even a major political decision or a profoundly significant economic event which it might be difficult to picture in detailed visual terms usually becomes news only when some man, in some physical setting, takes action. Let the reader see that action. It will read like fiction, for fiction is only an imitation news story.

III

To practice this kind of news writing not only leads to more readable stories, it also encourages a greater depth and accuracy in reporting. In this connection the following account from The

Springfield Leader and Press in Missouri is worth reading at
length:

David M. Oberman, stocky, bespectacled head of the Oberman Manufacturing Company, today attacked attempts to unionize his 1100 employees here by declaring formation of such a union would "force" him
to move his Springfield plant to Georgia. "Understand, I'm not against
the union," he said, "but we got to compete with non-union manufacturers, and if a union comes in here making demands, we can't do it."

Last night Oberman said removal of the plant, already started by the
dismantling of two units of sewing and pressing machines, would be
carried through to completion. Today, however, he said removal of the
plant "depends on my employes and the people of Springfield."

"How does it depend on your employes?" he was asked.

"They got to settle down to work, and stop cutting up," he said.

"How does it depend on the people of Springfield?"

"Do they want outsiders coming in here and putting out a lot of false
propaganda about how my girls are working 45 hours a week, instead
of 40? Do they want people like that to come in and tell us how to run
our business?"

"Do you mean the Chamber of Commerce should take some action
against the organizers of the union?"

"I'm not asking anything from the Chamber of Commerce. But
don't you think it's an injustice we should be forced to tear down all
this"—and he waved his arm to include the vast, four-floored factory—
"and put all these women out of work?"

Oberman said his "girls" had "asked me to talk to them today about
it" before taking any further action. "This I will do," he said. "One
floor at a time, I will talk to them, because we got no place in the
building big enough to hold them all. . . ."

A tour of the Oberman plant this morning showed it was all in
operation except for the two units on the first floor, which had been
dismantled yesterday, resulting in 150 workers being laid off.

Proudly, Oberman walked through his plant, explaining its workings
to a visitor, calling workers by their first names, receiving smiles in
return. At a lunch counter on the first floor, a crowd of girls were
drinking soft drinks or coffee.

"You see, it's recess now," explained the bland pants manufacturer.
"We work two hours, then we have a ten minute recess period. This
business is founded on truth and integrity and kindness. . . ."

Back at his private office on the first floor, three young women walked
up to him.

"Mr. Oberman," asked one of the girls, "is it all right for us to sign that paper?"

"Are you satisfied with your working conditions?" he asked. "Did you hear me say I was going to cut salaries? Are you getting $10.40 a week minimum and not working overtime?"

"It's that overtime," said the girl. You give us a certain amount of work to do to earn our $10.40, and they say get it out. If we don't finish it in eight hours, we got to stay till midnight to do it. And it's not our fault. If they get the stuff to us, we can make it up. But the line breaks down."

"Am I an angel? Am I marvelous, I could keep that line from breaking down once in a while?" shouted Oberman. "Once I got on a train and a coupling pin broke and I laid over in Indiana for 12 hours. Could I blame the railroad?"

More women gathered around, attracted by their employer's impassioned speech. One by one, in rapid succession, he turned to them, pointing his finger.

"Are you satisfied? Are you satisfied? Are you? And you?" he asked. The women nodded their heads in assent.

"The wages are all right," said the dark, plump girl who had spoken first. "It's that overtime."

"You don't have to work here, you know," said Oberman gently.

Back of Oberman, in the door of his office, stood J. W. Turner, head of a wholesale dry goods firm here. "Where would you women go to find a job if this plant closes?" he asked. "Don't you know Mr. Oberman is the one who supports you? Do you want to see this plant close and destroy the livelihood of at least 600 Springfield families?"

"Only this morning," recalled Oberman, "there was a woman with four children—"

"Five, Mr. Oberman," said a forewoman.

"Eight," said several others.

"Well, any way," continued the manufacturer, "she is supporting a family. Am I right, girls, that 50 per cent of the women working here are the breadwinners in their families?"

"That's right," shouted a chorus.

"I'm the woman, Mr. Oberman," said a middle-aged, small woman on the outskirts in the crowd. She was crying. So were several other middle-aged women in the crowd. The one who spoke was Mrs. Sarah Lister of 1810 East Central Street.

"I got five children. Seven mouths to feed. I've been working here 16 years. It's all I know. I want to work here. There ain't no woman going to set at a sewing machine all day, working hard, unless she wants to work—or unless, it's some young girl that wants to spend her money having a lot of fun."

"That's it," said Mr. Oberman. "It's the young ones that are doing all the talking. These older women don't want to see the plant close. They're satisfied. All of you who are satisfied, hold up your hands." (Fifty pairs of hands went up.) All who aren't satisfied. (No hands went up.)

"I'll talk to them today. Tomorrow, I hope, it should be definitely settled."

And he walked into his private office, with Mr. Turner.

The ordinary news story about Mr. Oberman's difficulties would merely state the general situation, give the comments of the employer and of a labor spokesman, throw in a few figures, and call it a day. This story, however, does not report from the outside in this fashion. It reports the thing itself, thereby allowing the reader to hear and see what goes on in Mr. Oberman's plant as though he were an eyewitness. This makes it unnecessary to say in so many words that the factory is a sweatshop. Mr. Oberman's tactics give off their own aroma and the reader knows the situation for what it is. That is why this kind of story fulfills the reportorial function deeply and authentically.

IV

To let the reader see the news itself may mean even more than reporting with depth and accuracy. It may mean the successful performance of a vital political function. If newspaper readers clearly see *das Ding an sich*—whether it is Mr. Oberman's pants factory or the inner negotiations of the Spanish nonintervention committee in London—they are more likely to understand it. This provides a more intelligent basis for public opinion; and in view of the far-reaching complexity of our present news in so far as it is of economic, political, or sociological import, an accurate basis for public opinion is more than ever necessary. Indeed it is not too much to say that the success of democracy under modern technical and industrial civilization depends upon it.

This is not to imply that American reporting, day in and day out, does not now give a fairly accurate picture of what happens. It does. Frequently, indeed, American reporters dig out news of public significance in spite of everything officialdom or the high command of business does to conceal it. An example is Paul Y. Anderson's report, in The St. Louis Post-Dispatch, detailing the scenes in the suppressed news reels showing police excesses in the Memorial Day strike riot in Chicago this year. All in all it is inaccurate to generalize about the inaccuracy of American reporting. It is probably the most complete and accurate in the world.

At the same time one cannot help feeling that the news of public and semi-public affairs is at times inadequate to the needs of contemporary democracy. As the organization and integration of human affairs has proceeded it has tended to concentrate control over an increasing area in the hands of those at the top. There has been no corresponding increase in the ability of the Fourth Estate to penetrate to the centers where decisions are made. The public does not yet know, for example, why Myron Taylor of United States Steel accepted the C.I.O. and why Tom Girdler of Republic Steel did not. It is not yet in full posssesion of the aims of John L. Lewis. Nor is this strange. The historic source of this kind of news has been some personal contact, some established channel between reporter and reported, and so it remains today. Yet it is difficult for a reporter assigned to a steel strike in Ohio to have the benefit of such a news source when half the story is made behind closed doors in Pittsburgh, New York, or Washington. The men on the job in these centers, meanwhile, lack the details of the scent available to the man in Ohio. The intricacy and multiplicity of sources of some of our major news events, in other words, sometimes make it difficult to maintain the reportorial function of presenting to the reader a clear view of what is happening behind the scenes.

It follows, therefore, that all too often those who have direct access to an important decision of industry or politics find in the newspapers only formal accounts, which skim the surface of the events in which they have participated. This explains in part at least an increasing tendency on the part of those in the seats of the mighty and near-mighty to look with distrust upon reports which they read of similar events in which they have not participated. It leads them to join the old refrain, "It's only a newspaper story."

It is extraordinarily difficult to penetrate the shield which under the present concentration of power those in control of our economic and political destinies place before them. I for one do not know how it can be done better than it already is—how, in other words, the technique of reporting Mr. Oberman's pants plant can be applied successfully to the inner workings of everything from the Republic Steel Corporation to the Fascist Grand Council. But at least we can see the need and state the objective: the increasing physical integration and technical complexity of the world have put new obstacles in the way of free access to the news, and it is essential that a corresponding means be found to enable the newspapers to report contemporary news as fully and freely as in the simpler world of yesterday.

This is only another way of saying that because of the apparently inevitable war that lies ahead in Europe, and because no one knows what forces are loose in this country, it is more than ever necessary for the citizens of the American democracy to see the news itself, so that they may understand it. It is up to the newspapers to let them see it, no matter what it is. Through their columns they must somehow once more bring to the people *das Ding an sich*. For whatever the structure of society, that is the function of the press.

Illustrations

SOME EXAMPLES OF
THE CHANGING AMERICAN NEWSPAPER

NEW YORK Herald Tribune

THE WEATHER
Today: Fair, slightly colder
Tomorrow: Mostly cloudy, warmer
Temperature Yesterday: Max. 47; Min. 31
Detailed Report on Page 20

VOL. XCVI No. 32,980

(Copyright, 1937)
New York Tribune Inc.

LATE CITY EDITION

WEDNESDAY, MARCH 3, 1937

TWO CENTS In Greater New York — THREE CENTS Within 200 Miles — FOUR CENTS Elsewhere

Vandenberg Backs Plan to Let Congress Curb Court

First Orthodox Republican to Speak Shows Workability of Alliance Against Roosevelt Plan

Sumners Implores Justices to Quit

Would Settle Whole Issue, He Declares in House; New Convert and Foe Come Out in Senate

From the Herald Tribune Bureau

WASHINGTON, March 2.—The first orthodox Republican to speak on the court issue, Senator Arthur H. Vandenberg, of Michigan, tonight indorsed the Wheeler-Bone amendment as a substitute for the President's court plan. He came had an immense importance as an indication that the alliance of conservatives and independents in opposition to the President is a workable one.

West Side

U. S. Delegation to Coronation May Include James Roosevelt

Choice for Secretarial Place Would Be Happy Thought, but It's News to Him, President Says

From the Herald Tribune Bureau

WASHINGTON, March 2.—James Roosevelt, the President's son and one member of his secretarial staff, may go to London officially to attend the coronation of King George VI, it was reported today. There is one post still vacant in connection with the American delegation to the coronation, and it would not surprise the State Department if the President's son were to go. Mr. Roosevelt, however, said that, while it was a happy thought, it was news to him and to himself.

Herald Tribune photo—Acme
James Roosevelt

Niagara Co. Defies State's Cut in Water

Power Firm, Ordered to Use But One-fourth of Present Supply, Cites Needs of Its Consumers

Demands Early Test Of Issue in Court

Refuses to Cripple Industries Served in the Western Area of State

The New York State Water Power and Control Commission has ordered the Niagara Falls Power Company to cut the amount of water it takes from the Niagara River from 20,000 cubic feet a second to 4,500 cubic feet, it became known yesterday.

Girl, 4, Is Slain By Attacker in Queens Mystery

Autopsy Reveals a Murder, Most Brutal in 27 Years' Experience, Official Says

Dr. Howard W. Neail, assistant medical examiner for Queens, announced yesterday after performing an autopsy that the death of Joan Morran, four years old, who died on Monday in her home at 119-41 Sutphin Boulevard, Jamaica, was caused by peritonitis resulting from a criminal attack.

---

2 Billion Secret In German Debt Bared by S.E.C.

Cautions U. S. Investors, but Allows New Bonds to Aid Previous Holders

From the Herald Tribune Bureau

WASHINGTON, March 2.—The Federal government, while permitting the issue of $80,000,000 of dollar bonds as the "only practical means" by which American holders of German securities might obtain "something of value" on their past-due interest claims, today publicly called attention to alleged "deficiencies" in the German registration statement and in effect charged the Reich government had a virtual "secret debt" of approximately $2,000,000,000.

Lewis Wins Steel Recognition For Bargaining; Roosevelt Asks Pay and Hour Law This Session

President Flatly States He Wants New Labor Legislation as He Submits N.R.A. Post-Mortem

Report Criticizes Impractical Codes

Suggests Future Efforts to Regulate Business Be More Flexible and on a Simplified Basis

By The Associated Press

WASHINGTON, March 2.—President Roosevelt came out flatly and emphatically today for new wage and hour legislation at the present session of Congress. He said at a press conference that such a statute ought to be enacted and that he hoped it could be before Congress gets through.

Behind-the-Scenes Steel Negotiators

John L. Lewis, head of Committee for Industrial Organization

Myron C. Taylor, chairman of United States Steel Corporation

Lewis Praises Taylor for the Agreement

Carnegie-Illinois Signs Contract Naming C.I.O. as Agent for Employees Who Are Members

Company Pledges No Discrimination

40-Hour Week and $5-a-Day Wage Effective March 16; Stocks Gain on News of Peace Pact

By the Associated Press

PITTSBURGH, March 2.—Organized labor won formal recognition tonight as a collective bargaining agent for its members from the chief unit of the United States Steel Corporation.

Steel's 40-Hour Week Hailed; Clears Way for Navy Contract

Washington Says Agreement Allows Industry to Bid on 25,000,000 Pounds for Warships; Accord Seen as Forerunner of Better Labor Standards

From the Herald Tribune Bureau

WASHINGTON, March 2.—The adoption of the forty-hour work agreement in the steel industry was hailed tonight by the Administration.

Detroit Strikes Close 2 Plants; 1 Makes Peace

Both Auto Firms Supply Ford, Revealed as One of Next Union Objectives

DETROIT, March 2.—Sit-down strikes closed two of the major parts plants in the nation's automobile capital today, but a settlement of one of the disputes was announced tonight.

Aviator Lacking a Gun Kills Coyote With Plane

Just Swoops Earthward and Breaks Animal's Back

ANCHORAGE, Alaska, March 2.—Pilot Jack Elliott, medical lecturer to aviation and remote native villages, told today how he broke a coyote's back.

Late City Edition of the

3 Cents

Gist

of Today's News

Vol. 96 No. 32,980 | Copyright 1937 Graduate School of Journalism, Columbia University | Wednesday, March 3, 1937

Harris & Ewing

Associated Press

THEY NEGOTIATED the steel agreement: John L. Lewis (left), head of the Committee for Industrial Organization, and Myron C. Taylor, chairman of the board, U. S. Steel Corporation.

Lewis Wins U. S. Steel Recognition, 40-Hour Week and $5 Minimum Pay

Labor

ORGANIZED LABOR has won formal recognition from the chief unit of the United States Steel Corporation. This epochal step was quietly announced in Pittsburgh last night by Philip Murray, chairman of the Steel Workers' Organizing Committee and chief lieutenant of John L. Lewis in the Committee for Industrial Organization. The agreement also provides minimum pay of $5 a day and a forty-hour week, both to take effect March 16. Eight other steel companies signed similar agreements, thereby probably preventing the major strike in the steel industry which many had thought inevitable this spring.

News of the agreement elated President Roosevelt and other Administration leaders in Washington. Officials of the Navy Department said it cleared the way for construction contracts which had been seriously threatened by the labor restrictions of the Walsh-Healy Act.

Unofficial opinion in New York steel circles held that the agreement will necessitate employment of 80,000 to 100,000 more workers in the steel industry at a cost of $100,000,000 a year. Prices of finished steel products are expected to increase from $2 to $6 a ton to compensate for the increase. On the stock market yesterday U. S. Steel rose almost $4 a share to 119 and Bethlehem $3 to 97½. Page 2.

A five-cent-an-hour salary increase was announced in Los Angeles yesterday by the Douglas Aircraft plant, scene of a sit-down strike which ended Monday with nearly 350 workmen under felony indictments. The pay rise was one-third that asked by the strikers. Page 3.

A properly-conducted strike "does not constitute duress," Justice Cotillo ruled in a New York County Supreme Court case yesterday, nor does the fact that a union contract has been signed as the result of a strike make his contract void. Page 2.

Today's Headlines

Roosevelt comes out for new wage-and-hour laws this session; sends Congress N.R.A. post-mortem urging new regulation of business be more flexible. *Labor, page 3*

Steel's 40-hour week hailed in Washington by Administration leaders; Navy Department holds it clears way for immediate ship construction. *Labor, page 2*

Sit-down strikes close two major parts plants in Detroit serving Ford Motor Co., which is revealed as early C.I.O. objective. One strike settled. *Labor, page 2*

Vandenberg backs Wheeler-Bone Amendment in radio speech attacking Roosevelt's court plan. Sumners implores justices to quit. *National News, page 5*

James Roosevelt may attend coronation of George VI as secretary of American delegation; President says idea is news to him. *Foreign News, page 5*

Niagara Falls Power Co. defies order of state commission to cut use of river water to one-fourth. *Business, page 14*

Mysterious death of four-year-old Queens girl caused by attack in "most brutal murder in 27 years." *Crime, page 9*

S.E.C. charges Germany has secret debt of 2 billion dollars; cautions investors in new bond issue. *Foreign News, page 6*

National News

SENATOR Arthur H. Vandenberg of Michigan endorsed the Wheeler-Bone amendment as a substitute for the President's Supreme Court plan in a nationally-broadcast radio speech last night. The amendment would permit Congress to override, by a two-thirds vote after an intervening election, Supreme Court decisions holding laws unconstitutional. In endorsing it and in praising the Borah amendment to enlarge state powers on social legislation, Senator Vandenberg became the first orthodox Republican to speak out on the court plan. Republicans saw in his action an important indication that conservatives and liberals could join in a workable opposition to the President's proposal.

In the Senate and House debate on the Court continued. Senator Hiram Johnson, California Republican, declared that any justice who withdrew under the new retirement bill would lose his self-respect. Representative Hatton W. Summers, Texas Democrat, in reply pled with the justices to do so, saying that thereby they would settle the whole issue. Page 5.

The Navy appropriation bill for the fiscal year 1937-1938, totaling $526,555,428, was reported to the House of Representatives yesterday as the first of the national defense measures. The money is to be spent for sixty-seven new vessels including two battleships at $60,000,000 each, for aircraft construction, and for an increase in Navy personnel to 105,000. Page 5.

The Treasury Department reported yesterday for the eight months of the fiscal year ended February 28 a deficit of $2,046,015,287, or $364,389,393 less than that for the same period last year. Receipts increased $368,427,542 and expenditures $4,038,149. Page 5.

Nine members of the Black Legion, including a former Mayor of Detroit suburb and a Detroit Board of Health inspector, were found guilty of a murder conspiracy yesterday. They joined more than twenty convicted in Michigan since the Black Legion murder of a WPA worker last May. The state's principal witness was Dayton Dean, confessed "executioner" of the terror band. Page 5.

Two earth tremors were sufficiently pronounced to rattle dishes and sway buildings in the vicinity of Lima and Bellefontaine, Ohio, yesterday. Other cities which reported upset furniture and swaying houses were: Columbus, Dayton, Zanesville, Springfield, Akron, Toledo, Canton, and Findlay. Five states surrounding Ohio felt the shocks but property damage was slight and no injuries were reported. Page 5.

Foreign News

THE Securities and Exchange Commission in Washington yesterday in effect charged the German Government with maintaining a secret debt of about $2000 million. It permitted registration of a $69 million issue of 3% dollar bonds as the only practical means by which American holders of German securities might obtain something of value on their past-due interest claims, but publicly called attention to what it called deficiencies in the German registration statement. Page 6.

James Roosevelt, the President's son and new member of his secretariat, may attend the coronation of King George in London as a member of the United States delegation. One post is still vacant and it would not surprise the State Department to see him go. The President said this was a happy thought, but news to him and his son. Page 6.

The Fascist Grand Council plunged Italy further into the world armament race at a meeting in Rome lasting until 3 A.M. yesterday. After listening to Premier Benito Mussolini it passed a resolution providing five lines of action toward further increases in Italian armed forces and economic self-sufficiency. In London a responsible report said Germany had tripled her air force in the last year to more than 2000 planes, with comparable increases in mechanizing its army of 830,000 men. In Toyko Vice-Admiral Saotake Toyoda, speaking for the government, said no increase in the proposed $342 million five-year naval program was needed because of recently announced British and American naval building plans. Page 6.

Foreign Secretary Anthony Eden rebuffed German demands for colonies by stating, in a speech in the House of Commons last night, that the Government was not considering any transfer of colonies. Thus he answered Ambassador Joachim von Ribbentrop's undiplomatic speech at Leipzig the previous day. Page 6.

The first serious movement by Germany to organize a world-wide resistance to the Communist International was made two weeks ago by establishing a bureau for the purpose in the Hotel Kaiserhof in Berlin, it was revealed yesterday. Meanwhile in Prague Dr. Kamil Krofta, Foreign Minister, declared before Parliamentary committees that Czechoslovakian-Soviet treaty did not make his country an "outpost of Communism in Central Europe," as charged in German newspapers. Page 6.

Seven hundred Spanish Fascist troops were surrounded during an attack on the Jamara front, southeast of Madrid, last night, a Government communique reported. The attack was said to have been repulsed with heavy losses. Page 6. . . . In Paris Niceto Alcala Zamora, who a year ago was President of Spain, was found last night, hard up and trying to make a living as a newspaper man. He refused to identify himself with either faction in the present struggle. Page. 7.

Crime

JOAN MORVAN, a four-year-old Queens girl who died Monday, was murdered. Death followed peritonitis caused by a criminal attack, Dr. Howard W. Neail said after an autopsy yesterday. He called it the most brutal murder in his twenty-seven years in the Queens medical examiner's office. Page 9.

The body of comely Cleo Sprouse, missing Charlottesville, Va., high school girl, was found near the University of Virginia cemetery yesterday by two students. Her head was tied in a chloroform-saturated towel. Page 9.

Two men trying to escape the scene of a Brooklyn hold-up yesterday afternoon made the mistake of commandeering a detective's car. One bandit is dead and the other lies under guard at the Kings County Hospital. Page 10.

Isaac Malester, cafeteria proprietor, was a witness for the defense in the restaurant racket trial yesterday. Under skillful questioning by prosecutor Thomas E. Dewey he became a witness for the prosecution. Page 9.

New York City

THIS YEAR'S summer city hall will be Chisholm Manor in College Point Park, Queens, Mayor LaGuardia announced yesterday. Page 9.

Embezzlement, slipshod financial conditions, and a political spoils system in the Kings County Sheriff's office under previous administrations were reported to the Mayor yesterday by Paul Blanshard, Commissioner of Accounts. Page 9.

At least 2500 more beds are needed immediately in the city's hospitals to care for tuberculosis patients, Dr. Haven Emerson declared yesterday. Page 9.

The State

HUGE CAKES of ice rumbled over Niagara Falls last night, jamming the river and threatening the Maid of the Mist steamers. Page 7.

In Albany the Federal Child Labor Amendment, already ratified by the Senate, was brought to the floor of the Assembly yesterday afternoon. Page 8.

Final passage of the Fischel minimum-wage bill for women and minors is scheduled for today in the democratic-controlled Senate. Page 8.

The Court of Appeals was asked yesterday to determine whether the Legislature has the right to prohibit alienation-of-affection suits. Page 8.

Business

THE New York State Water Power and Control Commission has ordered the Niagara Falls Power Co. to cut the amount of water it takes from the Niagara River from 20,000 to 4900 cubic feet a second. This became known yesterday when the company announced its refusal to obey, saying that to do so would adversely affect industrial concerns, traction companies, and homes throughout western New York. Page 14.

Senator Burton K. Wheeler, Montana Democrat, caustically attacked the past practice of New York Stock Exchange Governors in making decisions on securities in which they have an interest, at a Washington railroad investigation yesterday. Charles R. Gay, "new deal" president of the Exchange, testified how the Exchange is trying to meet criticism of this practice and of its listing of holding securities. Page 13.

Harrison Williams, husband of the best-dressed woman in America, was on the witness stand before the Securities and Exchange Commission in Washington yesterday. Commission attorneys said Williams' American Cities Power and Light stock rose 250% while its chief asset advanced only 25%. Page 13.

In Mexico City yesterday President Lazaro Cardenas set up a national petroleum administration. This will put Mexico directly into the oil business in competition with private industry, which includes approximately a $400 million foreign investment. Page 14.

Sale of the Gulf States Steel Co. to the Republic Steel Corp. was voted at directors' meetings of the two companies yesterday. Page 14.

Stocks: Steels, rails, and motors were leaders in a bullish but selective market inspired by the announcement of steel wage increases. Page 13. . . . **Bonds:** Corporate bonds generally followed the stock rise, but United States government issues fell somewhat. Page 13. . . . **Commodities:** Cotton continued advancing, closing 3 to 16 points higher. Wheat was unchanged to ⅞ higher. Page 13. . . . Foreign Exchange was dull and listless. Page 14.

Sports

Tennis: George Seewagen upset J. Gilbert Hall 6-2, 2-6, 10-8 in the national indoor singles championships here yesterday. Herbert Bowman and Frank Parker also advanced. Page 15.

Boxing: Max Schmeling arrived on the Berengaria last night with the intention of either fighting James Braddock in June for the heavyweight title or of suing for breach of contract. Page 16.

Hockey: The Detroit Red Wings defeated the Montreal Maroons 7-4 at Montreal yesterday. . . . The A.A.U. announced it would deny sanction to the Hershey Bears for their scheduled track meet if their hockey team played the disbarred Baltimore Orioles aday. Page 15.

Bicycle racing: After a session of wild jamming the team of Thomas and Reboli took undisputed leadership of the six-day race at Madison Square Garden last night. Page 16.

Baseball: Babe Phelps opened training at the Brooklyn Dodger camp with a display of heavy hitting. Mungo and three others hold out. . . . Danning signed with the Giants. . . . Dahlgren signed with the Yankees while seven others hold out. Page 15.

Racing: Miss Lizzie won the six-furlong dash at the New Orleans Fair Grounds. . . . Roman Soldier was withdrawn from as contender for the Widener Challenge Cup at Hialeah. Page 16.

Basketball: Columbia defeated Yale 41-37. . . . Thomas Jefferson won over Eastern District, 31-26. . . . Poly Prep defeated Trinity 31-16. Page 16.

Golf: Patty Berg won the qualifying medal in the Florida East Coast women's championship yesterday with a 76. Page 15.

Entertainment

Page 11

Books: Somerset Maugham's "Theater", for all its stage glamor and deft craftsmanship, is "plainly make-believe."

Theatre: Barre Lyndon's "The Amazing Dr. Clitterhouse" proved to be "a polite and gentlemanly melodrama."

Screen: "Outcast", a medical motion picture, demonstrates that even a good screen idea can grow stale.

Music: "Goetterdaemmerung" impressively concluded the Ring cycle at the Metropolitan last night, and the Oratorio Society's Bach Mass in B minor was again acclaimed at Carnegie Hall.

Radio: Cleveland Orchestra, WEAF, 1:45 P.M. . . . Mayor LaGuardia, WMCA, 2:15. . . . Opera "Lucrezia" from Milan, Italy, WJZ, 4:30. . . . Jessica Dragonette, WABC, 9.30. . . . Gladys Swarthout, WEAF, 10.30. . . . Newsboys' hawking contest, WJZ, 11.30.

Personal

Page 12

Married: Miss Vera Felicity Story and Henry Latrobe Roosevelt, in Philadelphia yesterday. Miss Dorothy Anne Day and Timothy F. Crowley, Jr., secretly in Greenwich, Conn., Saturday. Mrs. Dorothy Campbell, golfer, and Edward L. Howe, banker, in Elkton, Md., Monday.

Engaged: Miss Vivian Dixon, of New York, to T. Dennie Boardman of Boston.

Honors: Frederic William Goudy, distinguished type designer, will receive the Ulster-Irish Society medal at a testimonial dinner here March 19.

Deaths: H. H. Charles, 72, leader in the advertising field, of pneumonia yesterday at his home, 355 Riverside Drive. . . . The Rev. Warren H. Wilson, 69, rural sociology expert, following a mastoid operation yesterday in Presbyterian Hospital.

Weather: Fair and slightly colder today. Tomorrow, mostly cloudy and warmer.

An interesting experiment in news writing and makeup. Explained in the boxed story on page 2.

AN EXPERIMENTAL FRONT PAGE

The news of March 3, 1937, as published in The New York Herald Tribune on opposite page, translated into experimental form. The page size is considerably smaller, but it contains more news because the usual front-page stories are replaced by summaries of news from throughout the paper.

ORTHODOX INSIDE PAGES

Page 11 and (in lower right corner) page 10 of the same issue of The New York Herald Tribune as the front page shown on page 98. Some of the news stories are begun here, others are continued from page one.

Labor

Steel Signs C.I.O. Contract, Reversing Historic Labor Policy

The Setting

From the day in 1795 when South Carolina steel workers were paid $10 a month in bar iron, less $4.50 to the company for board, steel workers in America have struggled to better their lot. In 1892 came the bitterly-fought Homestead strike in Western Pennsylvania which Henry C. Frick finally broke with the help of Pinkerton men and the National Guard. In 1919 the National Committee for Organizing Iron and Steel Workers again sought to organize the rigidly anti-union industry. Reprisals by the management and the slowness of public sentiment to see labor's point of view broke that strike too.

Last June Philip Murray, first lieutenant of John L. Lewis in the Committee for Industrial Organization and chairman of the Steel Workers' Organizing Committee, set out to organize the steel industry. Supported by a $500,000 war chest raised by the Lewis unions, which have broken away from the more conservative American Federation of Labor, the committee has to date negotiated contracts with about thirty-six small companies employing 30,000 men. More recently its campaign turned against Big Steel—the United States Steel Corporation. This, plus recent aggressive C.I.O. activities in the automobile and other industries, led to fears that this spring would see the biggest and bloodiest strike in steel history.

What Happened

Day before yesterday Mr. Murray and Benjamin F. Fairless, president of Carnegie-Illinois, the biggest unit in United States Steel, sat down in an unannounced conference. Last night after a three-and-a-half hour continuation of the conference, Mr. Murray quietly announced that Carnegie-Illinois had recognized the union as bargaining agent for its members. Thus fears of a nation-wide steel strike vanished.

The agreement between Steel's chief unit and the C.I.O. union provides: "1. The corporation recognizes the Steel Workers' Organizing Committee . . . as the collective bargaining agency for those employes . . . who are members of the Amalgamated Association of Iron, Steel and Tin Workers . . . The Corporation . . . will not interfere with the right of its employes to become members of the union. . . . There shall be no discrimination, interference, restraint or coercion . . . because of membership in the union. . . . The Steel Workers' Organizing Committee . . . agrees not to intimidate or coerce employes . . . on corporation time or plant property.

"2. . . . There shall be an increase in wages of 10 cents an hour on all rates which are at present $4.20 a day, or a minimum for this classification of $5 a day of eight hours . . .

"3. . . . There shall be established an eight-hour day, forty-hour week. Time and one-half shall be paid for all overtime . . .

"4. A joint committee . . . shall meet not later than March 10, 1937, for the purpose of effectuating a written agreement on working conditions, application of wage rates, hours, rules and a method for adjudication of disputes. . . .

"5. The agreement . . . shall be in force until Feb. 28, 1938."

In New York last night, John L. Lewis issued the following statement: "The settlement is a fine example of an intelligent approach to a great economic problem. It has been made possible by the far-seeing vision and industrial statesmanship of Mr. Myron C. Taylor. From time to time over a period of several months, in New York and Washington, Mr. Taylor and I have engaged in conversations and negotiations. We were each conscious of the great weight of responsibility and the far-reaching consequences attached to our decisions. Labor, industry and the nation will be the beneficiaries."

Mr. Murray in Pittsburgh said that the agreement "paves the way for the maintenance of peace in the industry, and is in accord with the announced policies of the Committee for Industrial Organization and Steel Workers' Organizing Committee to organize steel workers without resorting to the use of strikes, violence or industrial disturbances. This agreement undoubtedly reflects the definite change in the labor policy of the United States Steel Corporation. We expect . . . organization of the entire steel industry."

Results

The wage-and-hour provisions of the agreement resemble those already announced by twelve other but smaller steel companies. With 120,000 men now added by Carnegie-Illinois, assurance of a $5-a-day minimum is held by 355,000 of the industry's 550,000 workers. The other companies, with the number of men involved, are: Bethlehem, 85,000; Republic, 52,000; National, 20,000; Youngstown Sheet and Tube, 16,000; Inland, 9,000; National Tube, 8,000; Pittsburgh, 7,000; and Sharon, Wheeling, Continental, Otis, and Jones & Laughlin, 25,000.

The New York stock market reacted optimistically to the agreement, with its probable end to the strike threat. U. S. Steel common pushed above 119 a share, a $4 advance, and Bethlehem common followed about $3 to 97½.

Unofficial opinion in New York steel circles last night held that a forty-hour week throughout the industry would necessitate employment of from 80,000 to 100,000 more workers while this, plus the rise in basic wage rates, will add more than $100 million to the annual steel payrolls. It was strongly indicated that formal announcements of price increases from $3 to $6 would follow before the end of the week. The cost of unionizing the industry, in other words, will probably be passed on to the consumer. It was feared that this may slow down demand at a time when the country's leading industry was gaining real momentum after five or six years of depression.

Washington Is Pleased

Adoption of the forty-hour week in the steel industry was hailed in Washington last night by the Administration as foreshadowing widespread acceptance of the Walsh-Healey Act's labor standards by other large industries.

The elation of President Roosevelt and Secretary of Labor Frances Perkins was shared by officials of the Navy Department. Charles Edison, Assistant Secretary of the Navy, prepared to reissue bids for the 25,000,000 tons of steel that the Navy needs to complete six destroyers and six submarines.

Deadlock Ended

Previously the steel companies had refused to bid on the Navy contracts because of the Walsh-Healey Act. This act, which became law September 28, specifies that companies doing business with the government must uphold the Administration's labor standards on any contract of $10,000 or over. It provides that workers' wages shall equal the prevailing local rate, that the work week shall not exceed forty hours, that no boys under sixteen or girls under eighteen years of age shall be employed, and that working conditions be healthful.

Mr. Edison expressed hope that manufacturers in other industries would fall into line with the Walsh-Healey Act's provisions, insuring the Navy the machinery and equipment it needs. Miss Perkins defended the government's refusal to exempt the steel industry from the act, saying that to do so would have weakened the Administration drive for better working conditions. President Roosevelt, asked whether a recent conference with Myron Taylor, chairman of the United States Steel Corporation, had anything to do with the steel agreement, smiled broadly and said that whenever he and his old friend Mr. Taylor got together they always talked about the welfare of the nation.

Sit-Down Strikes Close 2 Detroit Plants

Ford Next?

Sit-down strikes closed two major parts plants in Detroit yesterday, but a settlement of one of the disputes was announced last night. Both plants are sources of parts for several automobile manufacturers. They supply some of the requirements of the Ford Motor Company, which has been designated by the United Automobile Workers of America, a C.I.O. Union, as one of the next objectives in its organization campaign.

The main plant of the Murray Corporation of America, body manufacturers, was closed when 5,000 of the 6,500 employes struck (union figures). A few hours earlier 2,000 workers of the Motor Products Company had gone on strike, but the company reached agreement with the union by night.

The settlement provided immediate evacuation of the plant by strikers, "no discrimination by reason of the sit-down strike" reinstatement of four discharged employes, and a collective bargaining conference between Motor Products and the U.A.W.A.

General Motors

Meanwhile the same union's demand for a national minimum hourly wage was the only point undecided after nearly eleven days of conference with General Motors. Wyndham Mortimer, heading the union negotiations, said last night the union asked "equal pay for equal work, regardless of age, sex, color or locality." A General Motors spokesman said the union was insisting on "a uniform wage rate for all employes regardless of types of work, experience, skill, ability, sex, race or the geographical location in which the work is performed." The negotiators said they were still arguing on principles and had considered no definite figure for a proposed minimum.

The Fisher Body and Chevrolet units of General Motors at Janesville, Wis., closed since Friday by a strike, reopened today, returning 2,700 workers to their jobs. Near-capacity operations in General Motors units reopened since the paralyzing strikes ended February 11 were indicated in estimated production of cars and trucks at 123,874, the highest for any week this year and an increase from a revised figure of 108,617 for the preceding week.

More in Detroit

A strike closed the Zenith Carburetor Company, which employs 750, yesterday. Strikers demanded a ten-cent hourly wage increase, minimums of 70 cents for men and 55 cents for women, and a forty-hour week.

Sit-down strikers remained in possession of the plants of the Ferro Stamping Manufacturing Company and Timken-Detroit Axle Company. The Ferro strikers announced they would defend themselves "against violence and make this factory our graves if necessary." On petition of the companies Circuit Judge Allan Campbell ordered the Ferro strikers to show cause today, and the Timken strikers tomorrow, why an injunction against them should not be issued.

The Waiters' and Waitresses' Union which on Monday called strikes in two of Detroit's F. W. Woolworth stores, yesterday spread its activities to two of the city's largest restaurants. Fifty waitresses and kitchen employes struck at Stauffers' Washington Boulevard Cafe, forcing the management to turn away 250 patrons. The strikers demanded $12 for a six-day week, saying their present rate was less than $10 for a forty-eight hour week. At the Fisher Building sixty bus girls and boys started a sit-down in the basement concourse cafeteria. They wanted $10 a week, saying they now received $1.15 for a four-and-a-half hour day.

Meanwhile 100 sales girls passed the fourth day of their sit-down strike in the downtown Woolworth store, and eleven women clerks remained on strike in another store. The other thirty-eight Woolworth stores in the Detroit area continued business as usual. —ASSOCIATED PRESS

Other Strike News

Rhode Island Trucks

No serious disorder was reported from Rhode Island yesterday, first day of a strike of 2000 truck drivers. Police escorted such trucks as ran. State police, with all leaves canceled, patroled main highways. At least a score of trucks were turned back at the state line in Pawtucket.

Governor Quinn conferred with Thomas F. McMahon, state Director of Labor, to make certain that foodstuffs, fuel, and medicine was kept moving. He declared that while "the rights of the strikers must be preserved, . . . the public welfare comes before anything else."

Percy F. Arnold, president of the Commercial Haulers of Rhode Island, comprising thirty-five of the state's large trucking concerns, said that granting union demands for a 26 per cent pay rise would mean at least a 15 per cent increase in hauling rates, and that this would require consent of the Interstate Commerce Commission. "We might just as well sit tight and rot out of business as accept the union's demands and be driven out in thirty days," he added. —ASSOCIATED PRESS

Pennsylvania Hosiery

Three more hosiery mills in Berks County, Pennsylvania, were closed yesterday by sit-down strikes called in a unionization campaign of the A. F. of L. They were: Nolde-Horst Company's main plant in Reading; Reading Maid Company at Hyde Park; and Industrial Hosiery at Shillington. Union official said this brought the totals to ten closed plants, with more than 3000 workers affected.

Roosevelt Offers NRA Study As Basis for New Laws

Not 'Must,' but–

President Roosevelt came out flatly and emphatically yesterday for new wage and hour legislation. He said at a White House press conference that such a statute ought to be enacted and that he hoped it would be before Congress goes home. The President warned reporters, however, against quoting him as saying the legislation "must" be passed. He said that none of the legislation he has advocated is in the must category so far as he is concerned. The term has been used widely in the past to describe bills wanted by the President.

The President's move in the midst of his fight for power to name six new justices to the Supreme Court, where NRA with its wage and hour provisions was killed, stirred immediate speculation as to possible effects on that controversy. Some Administration supporters have predicted that labor groups would campaign unremittingly for the court reorganization if assured of new federal regulation of working conditions.

Shortly before the President came out for new wage-and-hour legislation he sent to Congress a post-mortem report on NRA which urged that future attempts to regulate business be simpler and more flexible. The report was written by the four members of the presidential committee on Industrial Analysis who are not government officers: Professor J. M. Clark of Columbia University, an economist; William H. Davis of New York City, a lawyer; George M. Harrison of Cincinnati, president of the Brotherhood of Railway Clerks and vice-president of the American Federation of Labor; George H. Mead of Dayton, Ohio, manufacturer and former chairman of the Business Advisory Council. Other members of the committee are the Secretaries of Agriculture, Commerce, and Labor.

Several of the committee findings drew a hot challenge from General Hugh S. Johnson, first NRA head, who said the group was packed with persons inimical to NRA.

NRA Report

A summary of the report compiled by the committee says:

"NRA gave jobs to something like 2,000,000 workers by spreading work. . . .

"NRA brought about a large increase in total wage distributions, which was at least partly neutralized by increasing prices. . . Average wage increases were moderate . . . the lowest-paid groups on the whole received the largest increases.

"The moral, and economic value of NRA child-labor provisions . . . is clear. . . . The public support given by NRA to the principle of freedom of labor to organize and bargain collectively was of great and probably lasting importance. . . .

"It is not possible to answer statistically the question whether NRA did or did not contribute to industrial recovery. . . . NRA attempted to cover more ground, and at greater speed than could possibly be covered effectively. . . .

"Both management and labor went too far, with the result that many impracticable and unenforceable provisions were put into the codes. . . . The apparently simple conception of fixing maximum hours, minimum wages and minimum price provisions developed wholly unexpected degrees of complexity. . . .

"The final NRA policy was, in spirit and intent, quite in harmony with the anti-trust laws. . . .

"NRA's field of action was one in which the public interest is obscure and the conflict of private interests is emphatic. . . .

"Many of the rules made, and which were supposed to have the force of law, were wholly devoid of the elements that make a law. They were uncertain and too complex to be understood. They did not have the support of that large majority of citizens upon which the enforcement of a law depends, but were such that all who were not in favor of them felt free to resist them. . . .

"Both for legal and for economic reasons, any program similar to that of NRA needs more definite standards than NRA possessed. . . . A minimum wage can be socially beneficial not only as a safeguard to the worker but also as a wage floor for the operation of the competitive system. But in this field code experience developed or implied the need of well-considered standards, which would be even more necessary to a long-run policy. . . .

"If controls of the NRA type are to be tried again, the experience indicates that the attempt should be limited to a few important industries in order that proper standards of investigation and adequate supervision may be maintained."

Cotillo Rules Strike Is Not Duress

Justice Salvatore A. Cotillo held in Supreme Court here yesterday that a strike legally called and properly conducted does not constitute duress. He overruled a report of a referee that a strike last fall against Beim, Ivler & Breiter, wholesale dress jobbers of 558 Broadway, was illegal.

The case goes back to April 16 last year, when an agreement was signed between the dress company and the Wholesale Dry Goods Employes Union, an A. F. of L. affiliate. Subsequently the union asserted that the employer had broken the agreement by refusing to pay its union employes for Labor Day, when they did not work. Ben Golden, arbitrator, favored the union. According to the union the firm refused to abide by this decision, whereupon a strike was called October 12. After two days the firm entered into a new contract with the union.

When later the firm declared that the new contract was invalid, Lorenzo C. Carlino, referee, found that the firm did not voluntarily execute it. Yesterday Justice Cotillo, however, ruled that the firm "may not thus repudiate an agreement entered into to avoid or settle such a strike." He pointed out that the strike may have been ill advised and unnecessary, "but it cannot be said it was illegal or in violation of the then existing agreement. . . . Having thus entered into the agreement and secured all the advantages of its terms until the expiration of the season, it does not appear just or equitable to permit the defendant to now repudiate it."

Douglas Aircraft Grants Pay Increase

Douglas Aircraft in California is a spectacularly successful designer and manufacturer of transports for commercial air lines

Continued at top of next page

The heads on these pages are in the Linotype Bodoni family, with body matter in 9 point Linotype Textype with Bold Face No. 2, and with Italic and Small Capitals, on a 10 point body. The box on this page is in the Linotype Memphis family.

These Pages . . .

are an experiment. Editorially they are the work of students in the Graduate School of Journalism of Columbia University, working under direction of Herbert Brucker, Assistant to the Dean. They have been set in type through courtesy of the Mergenthaler Linotype Company, and are being distributed to friends of the Graduate School of Journalism and as a supplement to The Linotype News.

As will be noted from the format and column width, the practical standards of newspaper work have been put aside deliberately. The guiding principle has been a search for a page size and news treatment suited to the needs of the newspaper reader under modern social conditions.

In order to provide ready comparison with standard practice the news published in the New York Herald Tribune of March 3, 1937, was used as a basis. The front page (see over) contains summaries of most of the stories which received top headlines throughout the Herald Tribune that day. The stories headlined on page one are the same ones displayed in the Herald Tribune's front page.

This second page is intended to serve as a sample inside page. Its news stories are the Herald Tribune or Associated Press stories of March 3, rewritten with condensation primarily in mind. Sometimes the standard news story form has been abandoned in the interests of simplicity, or to avoid repetition. Here and there related background material or interpretative matter has been added.

Comment and criticism will be welcomed. Please address Herbert Brucker, Assistant to the Dean, Graduate School of Journalism, Columbia University, New York City.

AN EXPERIMENTAL INSIDE PAGE

Much the same news as in The Herald Tribune opposite is here rewritten for a condensed and departmentalized newspaper, in a page size between that of tabloid and full size—five 15-em columns 18½ inches deep. The same information as in the standard form, and some background material as well, is given in about half the number of words. (See Chapter VIII.)

THE RICHMOND NEWS LEADER

Richmond's Greatest Newspaper

SATURDAY, JULY 3, 1937

The Week

DISAPPEARANCE OF AMELIA EARHART is distant Pacific waters gives tension to a holiday week-end in America...

THE SPANISH SITUATION presented to France a crisis of equal perplexity...

EMPLOYMENT OF THESE TROOPS brought a protest...

SECRETARY PERKINS, the governor, told the protesting delegation...

THAT BOTH SPANISH FACTIONS need suspicions is manifest from the virtual suspension of military operations...

A MAJOR SENSATION was created by this charge that a member of the President's Cabinet had urged the Governor of a State to detain the executive officers...

RUSSIA'S MARXISM seemed for a time this week to be threatened...

STEEL WORKERS were returning to the plants as the country on Monday...

GERMANY'S READINESS to take like advantage of the demoralization of Russia contributes to the quick breakdown of Mr. Stalin...

OUR STEEL WAR bristled with interest almost every day this week...

TWO HEAVY BLASTS of dynamite on waterways that fed the Cambria works shattered Tuesday morning...

PRESIDENT ROOSEVELT, on the same day that the watermains were destroyed at Johnstown...

CIO IS ON THE DEFENSIVE as the week ends...

NO CHANGE OCCURRED in the strike situation Wednesday forenoon...

WASHINGTON RIVALED the Chicago suburbs Thursday as an active sector in the industrial war...

THE ELECTION IN HENRICO on the continuance of county-manager government was the only after event of the week in Virginia...

THE NEWS LEADER FORUM

AN INDEPENDENT JUDICIARY: THE FUNDAMENTAL ISSUE.
Editor The News Leader:

THE FIGHT OVER THE SUPREME COURT waxed as the battle over steel slowly waned this week...

TO REDUCE HOMICIDE RATE: TREAT MURDER AS BAD.
Editor The News Leader:

THE VAST DEFICIT with which the fiscal year ended on June 30...

VIRGINIA RANKED FIFTH among American States in payments during 1936 to the Federal Treasury...

Bygone Days in Richmond

FIFTY YEARS AGO (1887).

TWENTY-FIVE YEARS AGO (1912).

TEN YEARS AGO (July 3, 1927).

A PIONEER WEEKLY NEWS REVIEW

In 1932 The Richmond News Leader abandoned its customary editorials in the Saturday editions, replacing them with an interpretive summary which places the significant news of the week in perspective.

Section 4

REVIEW OF THE WEEK
EDITORIAL CORRESPONDENCE
WEEK-END CABLES

The New York Times.

EDITORIALS
LETTERS TO THE EDITOR
SPECIAL ARTICLES

Section 4

E   Copyright, 1937, by The New York Times Company.   SUNDAY, JUNE 27, 1937.   E

THE NEWS OF THE WEEK IN REVIEW

HOW SOON WILL THESE CHIMNEYS BLACKEN THE SKY AGAIN?

Federal mediation failed last week to bring companies and strikers together. Chairman Girdler (left) of Republic Steel barred a contract with the C. I. O. and denounced Chairman Murray (right) of the Steel Workers Organizing Committee. At the top, guardsmen who kept order in strike centers, one of the struck mills, and demonstrating workers.

Right vs Right

To Strike—To Work

Mediators Meet

Steel Makers United

HE TOOK ACTION

Mr. Girdler Denounces

On the Strike Front

Johnstowners Protest

Ohio Mills Reopen

European Flare-up

Again Set off by Spain

Germany Quits Again

A Torpedo Is Heard

"Neurasthenia" in Berlin

THE NATION

Third-Term Talk

HE URGED COOLNESS

Nomination by Earle

Congressional Holiday

A New Champion

A STANDARD WEEKLY NEWS REVIEW

Since January, 1935, The New York Times has devoted the first two pages of its Sunday editorial section to an ordered summary of the highlights of the week's news.

The Buffalo Times

WEDNESDAY EVENING, JANUARY 6, 1937   PAGE 13

Tomorrow's No. 1 Bride

Holland's Juliana, who becomes Mrs. Lippe-Biesterfeld

It Really Happened:
Santa Visits Steel City Igloos . . .
Cops Forbidden to Talk Politics

Nation
President's Message

Abroad
Eden vs. Eggplant

Business
More probings

Orange-Nassau-Massowa

Medicine
Virus Blown Away

State
Still Fighting

Erie & Iron

Labor
Harvest of Words

Education
Prodigy, Goof

Sidelights

'The Lilacs,' Gen. Graves' Huge Home, Set an All-Time Record for Hospitality

Guest Invited There for Tea Might Stay Three or Four Days; Impromptu Theatricals, Parties Were Main Entertainment

By CARL WALL

The Lilacs, left, home of Gen. John Card Graves, which stood in Chapin Place.

The Large, Rambling House Stood Alone—'

Children Attend Nursery as Fathers Loaf, Mothers Work in Factory for Low Wages

Plant in Tennessee Industrial City Employs $5 to $10 a Week; Most of the Husbands Are Lazy, Irresponsible

By THOMAS L. STOKES

ROOSEVELT ACTION URGED IN STRIKE

Names Which Color Our Times

JEWISH FEDERATION WILL MEET SUNDAY

A DAILY REVIEW OF THE NEWS

In January, 1937, The Buffalo Times began to devote half the first page of its second section to this departmentalized summary of highlights of the day's news.

DAILY NEWS FINAL

BROOKLYN

NEW YORK'S PICTURE NEWSPAPER

Copyright, 1934, by News Syndicate Co., Inc. Reg. U. S. Pat. Off. Entered as 2nd class matter. Post Office, New York, N. Y.

Vol. 16. No. 115   80 Pages   New York, Wednesday, November 7, 1934*   2 Cents {IN CITY LIMITS | 3 CENTS Elsewhere}

THE WEATHER
Generally fair tonight and Sunday; not much change in temperature.
Additional weather data on Page 2.

No. 12,479   Entered as 2c Postoffice

LEHMAN LANDSLIDE

MOSES BEATEN BY 850,000

TAYLOR BEATS M'GOLDRICK

GUFFEY LEADS REED IN PA.

BULLETINS

Gov. A. Harry Moore (Dem.), defeated Hamilton F. Kean (Rep.), for Senator from New Jersey. William L. Dill (Dem.), was leading Harold G. Hoffman (Rep.), for Governor.

In 567 districts in New Jersey, Dill (Dem.) had 81,790 votes, Hoffman (Rep.) 83,919, with Democratic strongholds unreported.

TOPEKA, Kan., Nov. 6 (AP).—Returns from 243 precincts of 2,691 gave for repeal of State prohibition, 28,657; against repeal, 34,449.

BOISE, Idaho, Nov. 6 (AP).—The proposal to repeal the Idaho prohibition amendment was having a close race on early returns. Ten precincts of 792 gave: for repeal 745; against 729.

Hyde Park, N. Y., Nov. 6 (AP)—President Roosevelt learned with pleasure tonight that his home precinct had gone Democratic for the fourth time in history. It gave Gov. Lehman 449 votes to 376 for Moses.

Proposition No. 1, authorizing $40,000,000 Bond Issue to provide unemployment relief funds was winning by better than 8 to 1 in early tabulations. In 577 E. D. out of 3,847 in the city the vote stood: Yes, 86,065; No, 10,154.

The complete New York City vote for United States Senator was: Copeland 1,182,782; Cluett 384,252.

Lieut. Governor M. William Bray (Dem.) was leading his Republican opponent, Fred J. Douglas, by better than two to one, with more than a third of the State's election districts reported. The latest figures for 3,881 out of 8,591 election districts gave Bray, 1,099,269; Douglas, 481,986.

LOS ANGELES, Nov. 6 (AP).—Gov. Frank Merriam (Rep.) took a substantial lead over Upton Sinclair (Dem.) for Governor tonight, 425 out of 19,271 districts giving: Merriam, 44,179; nclair, 33,242; Haight (Ind.) 10,402.

Philadelphia, Nov. 6 (AP).—Senator David A. Reed, Republican seeking a third term, led Joseph Guffey, Democratic Roosevelt supporter, by 9,000 votes tonight, after nearly one-third of the State had reported. The vote in 2,524 of 7,957 districts was: Reed, 473,592; Guffey, 466,478. In 615 of 1,283 Philadelphia districts, Reed had 160,562 and Guffey 155,168.

BOSTON, Nov. 6 (AP).—The Boston Herald (Rep.) conceded the election of James M. Curley as Governor by 120,000 majority tonight at 10 P. M. The Herald was the only Boston morning newspaper supporting Gaspar G. Bacon, the Republican candidate.

Digest
Of Day's News

LOCAL
PAGE 1— Nine candidates for the House of Delegates from Richmond gave their views on four important questions before the public.
PAGE 2— Publication of figures showing greatly increased revenues from ABC stores during the past year brought forth renewed condemnation of the legal sale of liquor from officials of the Anti-Saloon League and the Methodist Temperance Board.
PAGE 2— With two persons, including one Richmonder, killed in automobile crashes in Virginia on the eve of the Fourth of July celebration, Director Rhodes, of the State Motor Vehicle Division, urged motorists to drive carefully to avoid accidents on crowded highways during the week-end holiday.
PAGE 3— Richmond women advocated the appointment of a woman to fill the vacancy on the Board of Motion Picture Censors, with Mrs. Emma Speed Sampson among those mentioned for the post.
PAGE 5— Mrs. Louise H. Zimmermann, widow of William H. Zimmermann, died today in her 82nd year.

GENERAL
PAGE 4— Repeated, faintly-heard SOS calls in Amelia Earhart's voice were heard as planes and ships speeded toward the spot in mid-Pacific where she was believed to be drifting when forced down on a world cruise.
PAGE 6— Colonel Jacob Schick, retired army officer and inventor of an electric razor, died in New York following an operation for a kidney ailment.
PAGE 9— Russia's official press began new drive against religion, charging churches are in league with fascism and capitalism in preparing for imperialistic wars.
PAGE 9— The compromise court bill gives Roosevelt what he set out to get, David Lawrence says.

SPORTS
PAGE 10— Mrs. Basil Coale, Richmond, scored a hole-in-one as one of the features in the State Woman's Golf Tournament. J. Nat Whitlow defeated Winston Montague in the first round of men's match play.
PAGE 10— Eddie Mooers planned to send Red Brandes back to short. Steve Mizerak to second, and Ernie Horne to third as the Colts meet Norfolk again after losing two straight to the Tars.
PAGE 10— Jimmy Mullen, Richmond's outboard champion, entered the Hampton regatta.
PAGE 11— The Cubs and the Giants were in the midst of a heated battle for the Fourth of July lead in the National League.

HEADLINES ONLY

An election front page of The New York Daily News, which has the largest circulation in the country. All detailed news stories are inside. See a further development of this idea, illustrated on page 99. The column to the right shows still another form of the same idea—news summaries on page one of The Richmond News Leader.

BOISE CAPITAL NEWS

Idaho's Independent Newspaper

Vol No. LXXVII—5 Cents   BOISE, IDAHO, MONDAY, JUNE 28, 1937   Telephone 24   No. 153

FINAL
TODAY'S
NEWS
TODAY

Flash, Flash!

Just waste its end and not one single word have we spoken about the lovely bride, the picture of beginners, the toast of the month.

So — with shakey hand — we describe the facts of male-selection for those swains who would have themselves sworn 'ere these hot fading June days the into hot July.

A girl's character is revealed by her legs, boys! If you are looking for one to marry, select one with long knees.

Ouch!

(BOPPO! We knew that would bring fire from our loved one.)

But those are the words of LeRoy Prinz, dance director for Paramount studios. Prinz admits he's a leg-watcher.

"I can tell a girl's character not only by her legs, but by her walk," he boasts. "I learn, a great deal by watching their intonation."

(Don't we all! Just watch a woman driving a car some time— the how much safer it is for you!)

"Intelligent girls lift their legs high when walking," Prinz-defying the world—continues. "Those possessing confidence indicate it by their free, forceful carriage.

"On the other hand, self conscious girls may be easily picked out of a line. They invariably walk with timidity. They cross the steps minomgly with short uncertain steps.

"Girls with firm knees and stiff legs are always of firm disposition while the careless girl is easily read by an expert who watches her dance for a few minutes. Uneven and slapstick steps furnish the clue.

Knees Know

"Round knees indicate an artistic temperament and talent, while Punky knees mean that their possessors are lazy. They will always be lagging behind.

"Knees that point outward reflect clumsiness, while hollow knees are a sure sign that a girl is truly feminine.

"Hard muscles that appear sharp when the calves are flexed tell plain enough that the owner is cruel and inclined to be querulous. Plumpness, on the contrary, indicates a good disposition."

Phooey!

A jab and a tusk for Prinz. We'll stick to the facial inspection method of determining with whom we will spend the rest of our life.

Beauty has a lot to do with fine women, don't you know.

But what's this? "THE GREATEST HINDRANCE TO GOOD ACTING IS — BEAUTY," our press-release informs us.

Once we knew a girl who was beautiful and also a good actor, but this is not the gist of the above statement.

Paramount's director Mitchell Leisen has this to say:

"Beautiful women especially are too often prone to be so conscious of their looks when working in a scene that they can't possibly lose themselves in their parts. But that frequently goes for handsome men, too.

"Give me plain-looking people in my pictures any time, rather than beauties who keep looking at themselves in the mirror between scenes. Always in front of the camera about their hair and their makeup.

"Even if they're unconscious of their beauty, it's likely to impress itself so strongly upon the audience that the full value of a scene will be sacrificed to it. That's why I use closeups as sparingly as possible."

Glamour Girl?

Should a prospective wife be glamorous?

No — glamour, according to Paramount, is still based on that old flossie definition, "A girl crazy by magic."

Thus a glamorous prospective bride is a bad hombre and should be avoided because she is a snake in the grass — or is she?

More about glamour:

"You'd may as well ask an electrician what a tornado is. Both that and glamour are mysterious forces in the world. They thrill and kill. But they defy analysis.

"The new Webster says that glamour is 'Any interest in, or association with, an object or person, through which the object or person seems more delusively magnified or glorified; a deceptive or enticing charm.'"

Finger

What about "figger" you ask? Here's reputedly the ideal "figger" although we expect, personally (Pruett!) it belongs to Eve West, herself:

Bust—5 feet 4 inches.
Bust—35⅛ inches.
Waist—27 inches.
Hips—38 inches.
Neck—13 inches.
Weight—115 pounds.
Shoe—4B.

Now, let us rest in peace!

Golf Tourney Tomorrow

Boise Kiwanis club members will take to the Plantation fairways for an 18-hole handicap golf tournament beginning at 3 p. m.

To the winner will go a trophy donated by Green-Griffin jewelers. Herschel Davidson will donate a dozen golf balls to anyone making a hole-in-one during the meet.

Slayer Of Three Surrenders In Chicago

Robert Irwin, artist and sculptor, surrendered in Chicago and readily confessed that he murdered beautiful Veronica Gedeon, her mother, and a roomer in their New York home. He is quoted as saying that his original intention was to kill only Mrs. Ethel Kudner, Veronica's sister, because he adored her and she married another man. Irwin is shown at the right, with Sheriff John Toman of Chicago, shortly before he was taken to New York for trial.

The News Today

Local

Joe Mulchler, pilot of plane which crashed into Nampa field, killing two late Saturday, didn't travel terms of any kind, acquaintances report. May fix blame for accident. Page 10.

Small crime wave strikes city over weekend—with police arresting two youths who confess to 19 car thefts since June 5. Break-in, crashes reported. Page 2.

Boise Masons return from Sunday trip to Idaho City where original organization was established. Page 6.

Surveys of irrigational possibilities opened with engineers in field to attempt completion of several major projects. Page 3.

Governor Clark proclaims Monday, July 5, official day for observance of Fourth of July. Page 3.

Idaho's second generation of Basques rapidly moving away from the customs of their ancestors, becoming thoroughly Americanized. Page 4.

First carload of new Idaho potatoes due to leave Caldwell tomorrow with prices a bit lower than expected. Page 2.

Building at three Idaho mental institutions nears starting point as plans drawn up and inspections completed. William awaits governor's approval. Page 1.

National

Federal mediation in steel strike collapses; mills operating near capacity; picket lines disappearing. Page 3.

Robert Irwin, confessed slayer of artists' model and two others, commits psychiatrist before releasing new confession. Page 5.

Three small girls kidnaped from California park, Inglewood citizens search surrounding country. Page 12.

War

Hitler gives world to understand Germany will not Fascists capture Spain.

Unidentified warships bombard Spanish coast.

Italian press blames Spain for attack on Italian warship.

(Spanish war, page 1.)

Markets

Stocks lower under load of rails.
Bonds lower; government decline.
Grains higher; wheat up 5% to 5% cents.
Silver in New York unchanged.
(Today's markets, page 15.)

Weather Report

For Boise and vicinity: Fair to-night. Tuesday partly cloudy with little change in temperature.

For Idaho: Tonight partly cloudy with little change in temperature.

For eastern Oregon: Partly cloudy tonight and Tuesday; little change in temperature.

For the mountains Tuesday; slightly cooler Tuesday.

Sun rises June 29 at 5:06 a. m.
LOCAL TEMPERATURES
The following temperatures were recorded in Boise during the past 12 hours:

2 a. m.	57	8 a. m.	52
3 a. m.	55	9 a. m.	63
4 a. m.	53	10 a. m.	72
5 a. m.	52	11 a. m.	77
6 a. m.	52	12 noon	83
7 a. m.	52	1 p. m.	88

Humidity at 1:12:45 p. m. . . 20

SUNDAY'S TEMPERATURES
Boise	93
Baker	80
Chicago	84
Calgary	92
Denver	84
Kansas City	86
Los Angeles	80
New York	82
Omaha	82
Pocatello	84
Portland	84
St. Louis	86
Salt Lake City	84
San Francisco	66
Seattle	72
Williston	82

Water Storage

ARROWROCK
Today . . . . . . 270,000 acre feet
Year ago . . . . 268,000 acre feet

DEER FLAT
Today . . . . . . 96,325 acre-feet
Year ago . . . . 132,325 acre feet

BOISE RIVER FLOW
Today . . . . . . 1780 second feet
Year ago . . . . 2966 second feet
40-year average . 3440 second feet

Final BULLETINS

Americans Advance At Wimbledon

WIMBLEDON, Eng., June 28 — Don Budge, Oakland, Cal., and Frank Parker, Spring Lake, N. J., moved ahead to the semi-final round of the All-England tennis championship today, but Bryan (Bitsy) Grant of Atlanta, was defeated.

Budge moved an easy win over Vivian McGrath, Australian Davis cupper. Parker followed with a close victory over Frank Wilde, No. 2 German rankings Parker and Budge will meet in the round of four.

Grant lost in straight sets to Bunny Austin, England's cup mainstay. The fourth place in the semi-finals went to Baron Gottfried von Cramm, Germany's ace, who will play Austin for a finalist's position.

Helen Jacobs and Alice Marble of California moved ahead to the round of eight in women's singles while Mrs. Dorothy Andrus of New York was eliminated.

Leaving Spain?

DOVER, England, June 28 — The German cruisers Leipzig and Koein and four destroyers passed eastward of Dover today, and a submarine was sighted off the Devonshire coast. They apparently were bound for Germany, causing belief here that the Nazis are withdrawing all their warships from Spanish waters.

"Skullduggery"

WASHINGTON, June 28— Rep. J. Will Taylor, R., Tennessee demanded in the house today a federal investigation into charges that federal officials are engaged in "skullduggery" and "rascals" by holding up "endorsing" prize copies of the Democratic year book delivered copies of the book as "dastardly skullduggery" and "racketeering."

End Inquiry

WASHINGTON, June 28— The senate patents committee today voted to end its inquiry into steel shortage at the plains of the Republic Steel company in Ohio without calling Postmaster General James A. Farley. At the same time it decided to refer charges of intimidation of employees to the La Follette civil liberties committee.

Claims Hughes Prejudiced

LOS ANGELES, June 28— William H. Neblett, law partner of Senator William Gibbs McAdoo, today questioned the eligibility of Chief Justice Charles Evans Hughes of the supreme court to act in the gigantic Fox Films Case because Hughes was biased in favor of the law firm he formerly headed and which his son now heads.

Soil Program

WASHINGTON, June 28— The senate today approved the conference report of the $500,000,000 agriculture department appropriation bill. The measure carries $500,000,000 for soil conservation activities, the $60,000,000 deducted by the senate having been restored by the conference board.

After The Wedding Ceremony

Smiling and happy after the ceremony that united them last Saturday, Mary Pickford and Buddy Rogers are shown with some of the many flowers that were used by well wishers. Miss Pickford, who is 43, has been married three times, but it is Rogers first trip to the altar.

Boise Calendar

Drill team of the Women of the Moose will meet in the Moose hall Tuesday evening at 7:30 o'clock. Members are requested to be present.

Kiwanis club meets at noon Tuesday in Owyhee hotel.

Rotary directors meet at noon Tuesday in Owyhee hotel.

Automobile dealers meet Tuesday noon in Owyhee hotel.

Junior chamber of commerce meeting at 12:15 o'clock Tuesday in Owyhee hotel.

Neighbors of Woodcraft will meet in the IOOF hall Tuesday at 2 o'clock to attend the funeral of Mabel Chris Alsip to be held from McBratney's at 3 o'clock.

Officers, guards and members of the Neighbors of Woodcraft are requested to meet in the I. O. O. F. hall Tuesday at 1 p. m.

Exchange directors meet at noon Tuesday in Hotel Boise.

Managers Make New Proposal

SAN FRANCISCO, June 28— Hotel managers today submitted "a new all-inclusive set of proposals" to striking hotel workers off the 10-day old strike against 15 hotels.

The proposals were presented to the San Francisco labor council advisory board which announced it would refer them to the joint committee of six striking unions for action.

R. B. Henderson, chairman of the hotel policy committee, said the operators offer several wage increases and preferential hiring provisions.

Temperature Hits 93; Boise Broils

Boise hit a new high in temperature Monday as thermometers rose to 94 at 1 p. m. and allowed every indication toward continued rises.

Predictions showed little change in temperatures in prospect for Tuesday.

Clear skies and a hot sun sent thermometers up to a new record for this season in Boise, beating Sunday's high by three degrees.

Approve Relief

WASHINGTON, June 28— The senate today approved the conference report on the $1,500,000,000 relief appropriation bill.

VITAL NEWS

MARRIAGE LICENSES
Gordon Paul Pemberton and Pauline Keith, both of Vale.
Arthur Raymond Hall, Nampa, and Florence B. Hawkins, Boise.
Andrew H. Burke and Dorothy Lucile Johnson, both of Boise.
Camino (Jay) Errington and Anna Marie Motchkowe, both of Nampa.
John Frederick Bashard, Austin, Ore., and Leslie Marie Davis, Boise.

BIRTHS
A daughter to Mr. and Mrs. Joe Bermanated, route 1, Boise.
Twin girls to Mr. and Mrs. William Donnelly, 1216 East State, Boise.
A son to Mr. and Mrs. William Lee Dyer, 1212 North 18, Boise.

DEATHS
Hawkins, Mrs. Ellen Elmira, 45, Boise, illness, at family home.
Alsip, Mrs. Cora Chris, 78, Boise, illness, at family home.
Lyons, Lloyd, 17, Twin Falls, illness, at hospital.
Champbell, Mrs. John F., 87, Boise, illness, at home of mother in Boise.

Making A Picnic Of President's Move For Party Harmony

Coatless, careless and completely informal, congressional Democrats gathered about President Roosevelt on Jefferson Island in the first of a series of party "love feasts." Here is the president seated at his ease under a big locust tree, behind him Representative Edward A. Kenney of New Jersey, and at right Senator Key Pittman of Nevada.

Sailing from the Naval Academy at Annapolis for the island in Chesapeake Bay, the congressional party was in high spirits. Here (top picture) are Representatives Sam Rayburn of Texas, Secretary of War Harry H. Woodring, Secretary of State Cordell Hull, Speaker William B. Bankhead, and Secretary of Agriculture Henry A. Wallace. A distinguished sea-going card pad on deck as the boat departed (lower picture): Senator James F. Byrnes, S. C., Robert J. Buckley, Ohio, and Pat Harrison, Miss. Returning congressmen reported that beer, juleps and fun were all on tap.

Caught by the lens just as he was about to speak, Postmaster General Farley is caught here speaking from the steamboat's deck as the cruisers, as informal as the spirit of the whole occasion.

CHINOOK JOE

Chinook Joe he say—

Square Crook, June 28.
Dear Newspaper:

Party of tourists from down country camping this week on creek near here. Them boys all bring out mosquito breaks. First local mosquitoes alloot one of squaw-crows, then came several pair of bald mosquitoes from Florida swamps, trucked by smell of fresh meat. Them tourists sleep at night, got fine chamber of creek there over the ridge and been four more pair from over that trail.

President Roosevelt felt this powerfully tame-looking crowd of real Democrats from all over country, all in shirt sleeves, having good time — and he figured as an informal as the spirit of the whole occasion.

CHINOOK JOE.

The Wisconsin State Journal

A fact-finding Newspaper

VOL. 149, NO. 4.   97th Year.   MADISON , SUNDAY, OCTOBE R 4, 1936   28-Pages   ★★★   Price Five Cents

Weather

Wisconsin: Unsettled and somewhat warmer, local showers Sunday or Sunday night; Monday partly cloudy. No extreme cold.

Home-Final Edition

University to Add Teachers; $20,000 Voted for Payroll

On the Inside

. . . there is no charge . . .

Drivers to Have Safety Classes
(Story on Page 3, Col. 3)

School Contest Winners Named
(Story on Page 2, Col. 4)

1936 Building Tops Last Year's
(Story on Page 17, Col. 1)

Budget Headaches to Start Monday
(Story on Page 16, Col. 4)

Marquette Defeats Badgers, 12-6

Northwestern ..18		Vanderbilt ..f...37	
Iowa 7		Chicago 0	
Illinois 13		Michigan State ..21	
Washington U... 7		Michigan 7	
Indiana 38		Ohio State ... 60	
Centre 0		N. Y. U. 0	
Notre Dame ...21		Yale 23	
Carnegie Tech ... 7		Cornell 0	

(Turn to the Sports Section for Details)

What's Behind Beggs Charges? Lid to Come Off This Week

By LAWRENCE H. FITZPATRICK

They Say Today:

Supervisors Discuss Grand Jury Study of Highway Probe

Liquid Fire Bombs Drop on Rebel City

(By United Press)

Norma Shearer Gets Better Part of $7,000,000

Background

Landon Tells Part of Lake State Route

TOPEKA, KANS.—(UP)—Gov. Alfred M. Landon Saturday announced part of the itinerary of his Great Lakes trip which will begin Oct. 4, and take him through the strategically important states of Illinois, Ohio, Michigan and Indiana.

Famed Versailles Chateau Afire

PARIS—(UP)—The famous chateau of Versailles, deeply interwoven with French history, caught fire Saturday night.

Youth Held Loser Through New Deal

CLEVELAND, O.—(UP)—Sen. Arthur H. Vandenberg, (R, Mich) said members of the Ohio League of Young Republicans Saturday night that the warfare will be given to a specific government.

Tragedy Brings Hint of Boat Inspections

In the wake of a tragedy, which Friday took the lives of four fishermen, and the subsequent discovery.

Man Killed, Grid Players Hurt in Crash

(Special to the Journal)
BLANCHARDVILLE — One man was killed, three minor members of the Blanchardville football team.

Plans Inquest in Car Deaths This Week

An inquest into the deaths of Nicholas Rapp, 28, Madison.

Badger Fans Happy Despite Hilltop Victory

Wisconsin supporters, somehow tired of sometimes-fickle, surprisingly found themself's displeased with the Badgers.

Ships Warned Out of Loyalist Ports

GIBRALTAR—(UP)—All foreign ships were warned in a broadcast.

Spanish President Bans Gold Export

MADRID — (UP) — President Manuel Azana Saturday.

Allen Says Borah Opposes Landin; Borah in Denial

BOISE Idaho — (UP) — Sen. William E. Borah Saturday night.

Move to Buy Reedsburg Bank

REEDSBURG — The Reedsburg bank will soon be a locally owned institution.

Cab, Car Crash; Girl, 15, Injured

Phyllis Pottiger, 15, of 20 N. Butler st.

September Rain Above Average

British Annex Eight South Sea Islands

LONDON—(UP)—Annexation by Great Britain of eight islands in the South Pacific was announced.

Woman Fails; Takes Life in Hotel Room

CHICAGO—(UP)—The body of Virginia Lee, 32, of Davenport, Ia., was found Saturday in her hotel room.

Merlin Stoflet 10, Hurt in Accident

Merlin Stoflet, 10, of 41 Wirth st., received a cut below his eye.

It Looks Like a Great Year for Co-Eds

Delaware Youth Lashed for Theft

WILMINGTON, Del.—(UP)—Clarence Lee, 21, received 10 lashes.

Noth Services to Be Abnormal

DAYTONA BEACH MORNING JOURNAL

VOL. XIII—NO. 82.   DAYTONA BEACH, FLORIDA, THURSDAY, DECEMBER 17, 1936.   Price Three Cents

TWO ARMIES CONTEND FOR CHINESE LEADER
(See Far East, Page 8)

Carpenters and Electricians Bolt Central Labor Council
(See Local News, Page 1)

HOPE FOR AIRLINER PASSENGERS GIVEN UP
(See Accidents, Page 2)

ACCIDENTS

Dies in Blast

COLUMBUS, O., Dec. 16—(P)—A terrific explosion in a downtown gasoline station tonight killed one man, injured three others seriously and wrecked the building of the Ohio Oil company.

New York Police, Firemen Break With G-Men

Taxpayer Protests Wallie's Flowers
(See England, Page 1.)

Klan Asks Curb of Miami Gambling
(See The Grower, Page 1.)

Miami Detective Chief Is Dismissed
(See Over the State, Page 1.)

Proponents Tell Why Canal Needed
(See Over the State, Page 1.)

Pardon Board Won't Hear Appeals
(See Over the State, Page 1.)

Seek $500,000 for Bethune-Cookman
(See Local News, Page 1.)

Fruit Shipments Limited to 500 Cars
(See The Grower, Page 1)

Law to Protect 'Gators Drawn Up
(See Animals, Page 1)

Glenn Frank Declares He Won't Quit
(See Education, Page 1)

F. D. R.'s Plan Wins Confab Approval
(See International, Page 1)

Pope Is Benefited by Day of Rest
(See Religion, Page 1)

Man Dies in Filling Station Blast
(See Accidents, Page 8)

FAR EAST

At a Glance

CRIME

Criticizes G-Men

SANTA CLAUS WORKSHOP

Dead or Alive

THE WEATHER
FLORIDA: Partly cloudy tonight and Tuesday, occasional showers on extreme South coast.
Barometer 30.06.
Ocean temperature 80.

The Palm Beach Times
24-Hour Leased Associated Press Wire Service, Also United Press

INLET TIDES

VOL. XV, No. 14   Today's News Today   WEST PALM BEACH, FLORIDA, MONDAY AFTERNOON, SEPTEMBER 21, 1936   Sixteen Pages Today   PRICE FIVE CENTS

REBEL ARMY VICTORIOUS ON MANY FRONTS
See Foreign Affair, Pag e 1

School Enrollment Here Up 10 Per Cent On Opening Day
See Local News, Page 1

FOREIGN AFFAIRS

Rebels Are Victorious On Many Fronts

THE WAR TODAY
By the United Press

Rebels In Alcazar Resist Stubbornly
By IRVING PFLAUM

Ethiopia May Lose Her Seat In League

OUR NEW STYLE

Today The Palm Beach Times offers a departure in the field of daily newspapers.

LOCAL NEWS

School Attendance Shows Increase

Cereus Will Bloom In Cemetery Tonight

Realtors Discuss Property Problems

Jury Studies Claim To Recluse's Estate

Freeholders To Vote On Bridge Tomorrow

Work On Airport

THE FIRST DEPARTMENTALIZED NEWSPAPERS

The front pages of two small Florida dailies, one morning and one evening, which were the first (October, 1936) in America fully to departmentalize their pages. Note department headings.

Religion

Japanese School Head To Visit Here

Niemoeller's Friend Arrested in Berlin

Mormons to Discuss Summer Work Plans

World's Hope in Church, Says Catholic Bishop

Louisa Minister Praised for Work

Georgian Elected President Of Presbyterian Association

National Affairs

Plan for 'Little TVA's' Called 'Cockeyed' Proposal

Senator Argues For Amendment

Huge Losses Laid To Supreme Court

2 U. S. Ministers Are Nominated

Tenancy Legislation Goes to Conference

Dr. and Mrs. Matsuta Hara of Kokura, Japan

Foreign Affairs

Bingham's Attack on 'Despots' Draws Fire of Nazi Press

Ambassador Bingham

Insurgents Forge Toward Santander

Russo-Japanese Situation Tense

De Valera Loses Majority In Irish House

Chautemps to Seek Fund of $386,500,000

Compromise Suits Eden, He Indicates

Friend of Duke Named British Ambassador

Swedish Prince Weds Commoner

Newfoundland Scouts Visit City Today

"LOOK WHAT A LOW PRICE Buys Today!"

HUDSON TERRAPLANE

No. 1 CARS of the Low and Moderate Price Fields

Save Money BUY YOUR NEW CAR THIS WEEK

FLEISCHMANN'S DISTILLED DRY GIN

COOL CLEAN, QUIET TRAVEL via ATLANTIC COAST LINE — AIR-CONDITIONED AIR-COOLED TRAINS

RICHMOND

Fifth Avenue Hotel

HYDRAULIC HILL-HOLD

A DEPARTMENTALIZED INSIDE PAGE

Early in 1937 The Richmond Times-Dispatch became the first larger newspaper to segregate all its news in departments. Note the department headings on this page: "Religion," "National Affairs," and "Foreign Affairs."

ALL THE NEWS ALL THE TIME

LARGEST HOME-DELIVERED CIRCULATION
LARGEST ADVERTISING VOLUME

MAdison 2345
The Times Telephone Number
Connecting All Departments

Los Angeles Times

EQUAL RIGHTS
LIBERTY UNDER THE LAW   TRUE INDUSTRIAL FREEDOM

IN TWO PARTS — 42 PAGES

Part I — GENERAL NEWS — 30 Pages

TIMES OFFICES
202 West First Street
And Throughout Southern California

VOL. LV   C   MONDAY MORNING, AUGUST 31, 1936.   DAILY, FIVE CENTS

Thousands Hunt Killers of Officers

Mob Apparently Bent on Lynching Trails Yreka Trio's Slayers

YREKA, Aug. 30. (AP)—Two law enforcement officers and a maritime pilot were shot to death at Horse Creek, isolated mining settlement near here, today in a battle with two prospectors, who fled before a rapidly growing citizen mob apparently bent on lynching.

Deputy Sheriff Martin Lange, Constable Joe Clark and Capt. Fred Seaborn, 50 years of age, a civilian pilot at the Mare Island navy yard, were shot down as they attempted to arrest John D. Bright, 33, and Coke T. Bright, 30, brothers.

POSSE ON TRAIL

The Brights vanished in the wilds of Horse Creek Canyon on buckbrush-covered mountain slopes thirty-five miles out of Yreka as a posse of officers rein-forced by angry citizens started after them.

Several hours later a Forest Service lookout reported seeing the brothers at Domnoco Mountain, twenty miles north of Horse Creek.

Placemen said they apparently are heading for Mt. Sterling, near the summit of the Siskiyou mountains, where they have a friend who doubtless will assist them. The posse was several miles behind them at the time.

BORDER PATROLLED

Two Oregon officers patrolled the State border, ready to stop the Brights if they ventured across the boundary line.

Yreka, scene of the lynching a year ago of Clyde Johnson, was virtually deserted as many of its 2200 residents deployed over the mountain wilds in the manhunt.

The posse, consisting of Sheriff Chandler, five deputies and two bloodhounds, trailed the brothers to Beil Meadows, at the head of Horse Creek, not far from the Oregon line.

Posse members said the Brights are armed with two rifles and still are in a killing mood.

The boulders and buckbrush made ideal hiding places for them and the posse moved carefully, seeking to cut off their avenue of escape into Oregon.

ARDENT ATTEMPT

Charles Baker, friend of Seaborn and survivor of the bloody battle, said the trouble started when he and the three victims

Turn to Page 5, Column 3

Head-on Auto Crash Takes Four Lives

MICHIGAN CITY (Ind.) Aug. 30. (AP) — Four persons were killed and six injured ten miles east of here today when two automobiles crashed head-on as they approached the top of a hill. The dead were Orange W. Barrett, 45 years of age and Fred Wayne; Mrs. Maude Barrett, 40, his wife; Roy Rohrer, 38, and Rarabelle Beitz, 22, of Chicago.

Six Chicago young people suffered critical injuries and were taken to a Laporte hospital. Automobiles expressed a belief that Mary O'Brien, 21, and Alice Kuhn, 22, were dying.

GOOD MORNING! MEET THE STREAMLINED 'TIMES'

We Trust Our New Type and Head Dress Meet With Your Approval

The Times presents a new typographical dress to the world this morning. Streamlined—it is the last word from the typographer's beauty shop and this newspaper trusts you will approve it.

The new type face which you are now reading is the result of exhaustive research carried on by the management of this newspaper for many months seeking a body type best suited to the eye of the newspaper reader. Gilbert P. Farrar, typography expert for the American Type Founders Corporation, acted as counselor in the experimental work.

MODERN GOTHIC HEADS

The heads are from the modern Gothic family and designed to enhance legibility and at the same time give the copyreader an opportunity to tell the story and not devote the major portion of his efforts in searching for a combination of words to balance and fit a certain space. If white space results—so much the better. Air—white space—is restful to the eye and aids in the reading of a page.

In case you have forgotten, this paragraph is set in the body type used by The Times today. Previously, newspapers have discovered this type to be too small for the text type of any newspaper, and the managements of the newspapers believe the readers will appreciate the change.

The new text type is Paragon eight point set on a nine point base. The old type was a seven point set on an eight point base. Thus the body type will be a point larger in size than the old and set on a point wider base. Both of these features, of course, add to the ease with which the eye can scan the type.

PHONES TO WIFE

It was almost nine hours after his ship struck the ground, traveling at terrific speed, before he was given medical aid. It was then he telephoned his wife, Mrs. Carline Turner, 2303 Hobby-ridge Drive, who was almost prostrate with anxiety over his mysterious disappearance.

"He was very nervous and excited," said Mrs. Turner, who received word from her husband at 6:45 p.m. "He told me he would

Turn to Page 5, Column 5

Envoy-Bride Quits Post

Bryan Daughter's Resignation Disclosed on Roosevelt Train

RAPID CITY (S. D.) Aug. 30. (AP)—Ruth Bryan Owen Rohde has resigned as Minister to Denmark, it was announced today aboard President Roosevelt's special train.

Mrs. Rohde, America's first woman diplomat, and daughter of the late William Jennings Bryan, recently married Capt. Boerje Rohde of the King of Denmark's personal bodyguards, at St. James Episcopal Church in Hyde Park, N. Y. The President and Mrs. Roosevelt attended the ceremony.

ACTION EXPECTED

At that time it was expected the resignation would be forthcoming in view of the fact Mrs. Owen had become the wife of a foreigner. The couple now is in the United States on a honeymoon.

The following exchange of telegrams was given out:

"Mr. President; desiring to

Turn to Page 5, Column 4

Fiery Plane Kills One and Hurts Three

NEW YORK, Aug. 30. (AP)—A private plane crashed in flames in the midst of a group of Sunday picnickers today at Farm Point, Long Island Sound, killing one woman and injuring three other persons.

The plane was destroyed by fire and two occupants escaped injury.

Sylvia Saimi, 29 years of age, of Manhattan, was killed.

In the plane were Herbert S. Rose of the Bronx, a commercial pilot, and Robert Ferguson of the Bronx, a student flyer.

Col. Turner Crashes in New Mexico

Speed Pilot Seriously Injured in Wreck of Bullet-like Ship

His 1000-horsepower speed plane a tangled wreck on the desert wasteland sixty-five miles south of Gallup, N. M., Col. Roscoe Turner, with several ribs broken, was aboard the Santa Fe Chief last night en route to Los Angeles.

He will be taken from the train at 1:30 p.m. on a litter, his hopes shattered of winning the 1936 Bendix transcontinental race, for which he holds the record.

SHIP WRECKED

Turner's bullet-shaped ship, in which he took off from Union Air Terminal at 5:30 yesterday morning, was demolished in a forced landing at 9 a.m. on the edge of the Zuni Reservation.

His throttle broke, cutting off his engine and forcing him down in the inaccessible and sparsely populated mountain district at Gallup, he said, after he had ridden eighteen miles on a horse given him by Zuni Indians and then had taken an automobile into town.

BROKEN RIBS

Speaking from his hotel room he said he does not know just what is the matter with him but that he thinks he had some broken ribs. He was put aboard the Chief at 8:30 p.m.

Asked how badly his plane was damaged, he said:

"Bad enough that I'll just take the motor out and leave the rest of it there."

The scene of the mishap is approximately 180 miles west of Albuquerque and a few miles west of the Zuni mountain range, which, as the Continental Di-vide, towers more than 8000 feet at the point near the crash.

County Tax Rate Raised to $1.27 for Each $100

Los Angeles county's final budget for 1936-37 carrying a flat rate for proposed expenditures that will necessitate a minimum tax rate of $1.27 on each $100 of assessed valuation, 8 cents higher than last year, was adopted by the Board of Supervisors shortly before midnight last night, the time limit in which action could be taken.

As the budget stands after an analysis by a force of accountants in County Auditor Payne's department, the total to be raised by taxation is approximately $29,500,000, the top of this figure is approximately $19,000,000 more, this amount being paid in various revenues received by the county throughout the year.

The 8 cents increase over the $1.19 rate of last year is due primarily to two items. One item was the sum of $1,500,000 which had to be set up to meet a judgment recently obtained by the county in the several suits filed by the board tomorrow.

Turn to Page 5, Column 3

APPEAL VOICED BY POPE PIUS

Prayers of Pilgrims Urged to Save World

CASTEL GANDOLFO (Italy) Aug. 30 (AP)—Pope Pius XI urged a group of pilgrims tonight to pray "lest the continued atrocities of men" result in "grave affliction for fallen humanity."

Speaking to thirty Italians who came to pay him homage, the Pope, weakened by worry over the Spanish war, thanked them for coming to see "the father who not only grows older but is, in deed, sad."

His seventy-nine years, he said, "are an imposing number and provoke many preoccupations."

After chatting briefly with the pilgrims, the Holy Father turned sadly to the theme which has harassed him in recent days.

"We thank you for your promise to continue your prayers, of which we have need with such distances shadows which have put such menaces to hope for the mercy of God lest also to fear—with the continued atrocities of men—lest menaces against fallen humanity."

Spanish Plane Rains Bombs at United States Destroyer

U.S.S. Kane Returns Fire; Hull Warns Both Sides at Order of Roosevelt

WASHINGTON, Aug. 30. (AP)—An American destroy-er—the U.S.S. Kane—was the target for air bombs from an unidentified monoplane off the coast of Spain today, and tonight a protest was being prepared for dispatch to both the Spanish government and the Spanish rebels.

The destroyer was not hit. It fired nine rounds from its anti-aircraft gun at the airplane flew away apparently without harm.

President Roosevelt by long distance telephone from Rapid City, S. D., directed Secretary of State Hull to frame the protests. The incident was brought to the attention of both participants in the civil war in Spain immediately through the American Embassy at Madrid.

Secretary Hull was at work tonight drafting formal representations.

The State Department said both sides will be asked to "issue instructions in the strongest terms" to both sides to "prevent another incident of this character."

The department made it plain it considered the bombing the result of mistaken identity of the American ship.

"Since both the government forces and the opposing forces in Spain in the friendliest spirit have made every possible effort to avoid injury to American na-tionals and American property," the department's statement said, "it can only be assumed that the attack on the United States de-stroyer Kane was due to the iden-tity having been mistaken by a pilot of one faction for a ves-sel of the other."

AMERICAN STATEMENT

The Department's statement: "The United States destroyer Kane left Gibraltar at 8:12 Au-gust 30 en route to Bilbao, Spain, to assist in the work of evacu-ating American nationals from Spain. It will be recalled that since the inception of the pres-ent conflict in Spain, the Ameri-can government has repeatedly urged all American nationals to proceed from Spain to places of safety and has provided vessels to remove them from Spanish ports.

"We must be strong! N's must be always strongest! We must be so strong that we can face any eventualities and look directly to the eye whatever may befall!"

It was here the slender pontiff spoke of his anxiety regarding the war and of his earlier dreams of peace.

"According to a report from the commanding officer of the United States destroyer Kane, at 4:35 p.m. (Spanish time) Au-gust 30, at 38 degrees 10 minutes North, 7 degrees, 33 minutes West, approximately forty miles off the Spanish coast, an uniden-tified tri-motored, low-winged monoplane flew over the Kane and dropped two bombs which exploded near the vessel.

DUCE GIVES War Warning to World

Copyright, 1936, by the Associated Press

AVELLINO (Italy) Aug. 30 Italy's Mussolini warned a re-arming world tonight that one million 8,000,000 soldiers in the course of a few hours and after a simple order.

Speaking from this heart of rustic wine and pig fisheries and his people, the dictator rejected what he called "the stu-pidity of eternal peace," de-clared its army was sharpened up by its African victory, and pro-claimed:

ROOSEVELT DEDICATES HUGE MEMORIAL TO JEFFERSON

RAPID CITY (S. D.) Aug. 30 —The tall Black Hills of South Dakota President House of Washington President Roosevelt today dedicated the Thomas Jefferson figure on the huge Mount Rushmore Memorial. The monument which he said "can be completed only when we reach government, not only in our own country, but, we hope, through-out the world."

From a right far below the huge memorial, where the busts of Washington, Jefferson, Lin-coln and Theodore Roosevelt are to be chiselled from a rocky cliff, he saw the thundering blasts of dynamite send tons of rock hurl-ing down the mountainside.

The saw a seventy-foot Ameri-can flag drawn from the half-completed figure of the third

Turn to Page 5, Column 3

HUNTING FOR TROUBLE

Col. Roscoe Turner, who crashed yesterday in New Mex-ico, shown looking for motor trouble after he narrowly missed crashing at the airport Saturday.

Times photo

Korean Typhoon Leaves 1104 Dead and 426 Missing

TOKIO (Monday) Aug. 31. (UP)—The Korean government announced today that 1104 per-sons were killed by a typhoon which struck Southern Korea Saturday. In addition, 1926 per-sons were injured and 426 were reported missing.

The gale has subsided and Korea was recording. All foreign-ers were believed safe.

Second Lightning Bolt Burns Barn

STERLING (Ill.) Aug. 30. (Ex-clusive)—Thursday night light-ning struck the Frank Mitchell barn near Mount Carroll with little damage. Last night light-ning again struck the barn and sadly to the theme which has harassed him in recent weeks.

Soviet Troops Spurn Orders in Passive Rebellion

MOSCOW, Aug. 30. (Exclu-sive)—A passive revolt among Red army troops at Rizan who refused to obey their officers subsided under the unrest re-sulting from the government's drastic action in purging anti-Stalin elements and hunger for-merly connected with Leon Trotsky, exiled Red army head.

The disturbances at Rizan was quickly "reduced" by army authorities. It was reported. Re-ports continued to reach Mos-cow, however, of open anti-gov-ernment agitation by peasants in the Ukraine, where troops of

said to have received extremely severe orders to stamp out the protests.

Rizan, about 200 miles from the capital, is a post center where the troops were rushed recently to fight fires in the peat fields. Many victims were taken by the fires.

The government tonight or-dered an undisclosed number of functionaries and civil work-ers in Moscow and the prov-inces as a result of the "Trotsky trial" at which sixteen persons were executed after being con-victed of plotting to set up a "regime of terror."

Alfonso's Son Reported Better

NEW YORK, Aug. 30.—(AP)— Physicians attending the Count of Covadonga, former Crown Prince of Spain, reported today he spent a comfortable night at his bedside in the hospital where he was taken after an auto-mobile accident Friday.

The Count, son of former King Alfonso, suffering from hemophilia, the Count was taken to the hospital after a hemor-rhage that followed the injuring

SPOKANE MARKS STREET CAR'S PASSING TODAY

SPOKANE (Wash.) Aug. 30. (AP)—Spokane tomorrow will celebrate the ending of street railway traffic here.

The high light of the program will be the public burning of one of the last of the rattling trol-ley cars.

OBSERVATIONS

By Irvin S. Cobb

SANTA MONICA, Aug. 30. Local travel increase report an increase of incoming tourists. But then again on the other hand, part of it may be due to returning residents who were hurrying to avoid when the papers started printing a certain re-markble diary. If your soul does not always find you out at least they frequently find you getting out.

It's all over now and peace

and quiet have been restored to our home-circles, but at the height of the rush one involuntarily was reminded of the ancient story of the Freshman who fox with his friend he could prove every man, however outworld pure, had a dreaded secret in his past. So he sent to six different persons one of these anonymous tele-grams, reading merely, "Flee at once—all is discovered!"

Promptly five of the six took the midnight train for parts unknown, leav-ing no forwarding address. But, of course, this was just to prove before us. It couldn't really happen here.

IRVIN S. COBB

Copyright, 1936, by Mc Naught Newspaper Syndicate

MODERN NEWSPAPER TYPOGRAPHY

Although most newspapers retain the conservative typography exemplified by The New York Herald Tribune (see page 98), there is a growing tendency to adopt sans-serif display type, simplified headlines set flush at left, and larger body type. All are shown in The Los Angeles Times above. This paper won the 1937 Ayer award for newspaper typography.

NEW YORK ★★★★★★★ 7TH FINAL
BASEBALL . . . RACING

EVENING Journal

No. 18,077—DAILY MONDAY, MAY 24, 1937 Average Daily Net Paid Circulation for April, 1937 642,185 3 CENTS

LINDYS HAVE SON

MRS. LINDBERGH COL. LINDBERGH

Residents of England since the conviction and execution of Bruno Richard Hauptmann for the kidnaping and murder of their first baby, Col. and Mrs. Charles A. Lindbergh are the parents of another son. The infant was born on coronation day in Weald, a few miles north of London, according to relatives.

COURT UPHOLDS SECURITY ACT

WASHINGTON, May 24 (By International News Service).—In three epochal decisions, two by the narrow margin of 5 to 4, the Supreme Court today held constitutional the Administration's vast social security program and also the right of 45 states to enact unemployment insurance laws.

Associate Justice Benjamin N. Cardozo, observing his 67th birthday today, delivered two of the opinions, while Justice Stone delivered the third.

The decisions were:

1. Court held constitutional the old-age annuity tax of the Federal social security law, affecting 27,000,000 workers and 2,500,000 employers, by a 7 to 2 vote. Justices McReynolds and Butler dissented.

2. Court upheld Federal unemployment insurance payroll tax provisions of Federal Social Security Act, together with administrative provisions designed to assure enactment of unemployment insurance laws in every State. Forty-five States

Continued on Page 10, Column 1.

VERY LATEST NEWS

BASEBALL SCORES

Cleveland (A). 0 0 0 0 0 0 0
Yankees (A)... 0 0 0 8 4 0
Batteries—Andrews and Pytlak; Chandler and Dickey.
Giants (N).... 0 0 0 0 2 0
Pittsburg (N). 0 1 0 0 0 0
Batteries—Hubbell and Mancuso; Brandt and Todd.
Dodgers (N). 0 1 0 0
Cincinnati (N) 0 0 0 0
Batteries—Butcher and Phelps; L. Moore and V. Davis.
Boston (N)... 1 0 0
Chicago (N).. 0 1 0
Batteries—Fette and Lopez; Carleton and Hartnett.
St. Louis (A). 0 1 1 0 0 2
Phila (A)..... 2 1 1 0 2 0
Batteries—Thomas and Hemsley; Nelson and Hayes.

Chicago (A).. 0 0 3 0 1 0
Boston (A)... 2 0 2 1 4 0
Batteries—Rigney and Sewell; Walberg and Desautels.
Detroit (A)... 0 2
Wash'ton (A). 1 0
Batteries—Lawson and Cochrane; Newson and Millies.
Newark (I)... 3 1 2 0 2
Jersey City (I) 0 1 3 0 0
Batteries—Brown & Hershberger: Babich & Redmond.
Second Game—
Rochester (I). 0 0 0 0 0 0 0 0 0—0 5 2
Toronto (I)... 2 0 0 0 0 0 0 0 x—2 4 0
Batteries—Judd and O'Farrell: Meola and Heath.
Second Game—
Buffalo (I)... 0 0 1 0
Montreal (I).. 0 0 0 1
Batteries—Ash and Savino; Smythe and Stephenson.

At Potsdam, N. Y.—End 5th—Hartwick Col. 4, Clarkson 0.
At Brunswick, Me.—End 6th—Colby 2, Bowdoin 5.
At Fordham Field—C. C. N. Y., 0, Fordham 0.
At Reading, Pa.—Moravian 6, Albright 1.

RACING RESULTS

AT BELMONT PARK.

Fifth—Round Table 11-5, 4-5, 1-3; Iron Ore 1-1, 2-5; Fight Talk 3-1. Off 4:24½.
Sixth—Glittering 8-5, 1-3, out; Wilco 1-4, out; Syriac 1-3. Off 4:47.
Scratched—Hymn.

AT WOODBINE.

Fifth—Sam Worthy 21.65, 8.40, 5.95; Sweepden 10.75, 5.90; Worthy Duke 5.55. Off 4:48.
Scratched—Lady Much.

AT BEULAH PARK.

Third—Perdition 7.00, 3.80, 3.00; Squeeze Out 4.40, 2.80; Blind Star 4.00. Off 4:31.

AT SUFFOLK DOWNS.

Fifth—Mucho Gusto 6.20, 3.40, 2.60; Lady Higloss 3.60, 3.00; Weston 3.20. Off 4:36½.
Scratched—Rudie, S. Advice, New Deal, Zoic, Accolade.

AT WASHINGTON PARK.

Fourth—Conrad Mann 6.40, 4.00, 2.60: Night Bandit 4.80, 2.60; Tedsim 2.40. Off 4:39.

THE WEATHER

Clear or partly cloudy this afternoon, tonight and tomorow. Continued warm.

Sun rises, 5:32 a. m.; sun sets, 8:14 p. m. High tide at Governors Island, 8:45 a. m. and 8:53 p. m.

(Complete Weather Table on Page 2.)

U. S. TREASURY REPORT.
(Figures in Financial Section.)

7-Inch Trout Legal

ALBANY, May 24 (By International News Service).—Gov. Lehman announced today that on Tuesday, June 1, he will sign the Pease Bill increasing from six to seven inches the legal size at which trout may be taken.

The bill, which is State-wide in application, will become effective as soon as it is signed.

Wage, Hour Law Asked

Hubbell, After 23rd Straight, Faces Bucs

BATTING ORDER.

GIANTS	PITTSBURGH
Bartell, ss	Jensen, cf
Chiozza, 3b	P. Waner, rf
Moore, lf	Dickshot, lf
Ripple, cf	Vaughan, ss
Ott, rf	Suhr, 1b
McCarthy, 1b	Todd, c
Mancuso, c	Handley, 2b
Whitehead, 2b	Brubaker, 3b
Hubbell, p	Brandt, p

Umpires—Moran, Magerkurth and Parker.

By Garry Schumacher.

FORBES FIELD, Pittsburgh, May 24. — Pittsburgh paid Carl Hubbell a nice tribute here this afternoon when 12,000 fans, one of the biggest Monday crowds in years, piled into Forbes Field to watch the screw ball master pitch

Continued on Page 23.

Butcher in Box for Dodgers

BATTING ORDER.

BROOKLYN	CINCINNATI
Brack, rf	Jordan, 1b
Lavagetto, 2b	Goodman, rf
Cooney, cf	Cuyler, cf
Hassett, 1b	Hafey, lf
Winsett, lf	V. Davis, c
Phelps, c	Outlaw, 3b
English, ss	Gelbert, ss
Stripp, 3b	Kampouris, 2b
Butcher, p	Moore, p.

Umpires—Ballanfant, Klem and Sears.

By Stan Lomax.

REDLAND FIELD, CINCINNATI, May 24.—Big Max Butcher, shelled from the mound by the Cardinals in his last start, came back again this afternoon when the Brooklyn Dodgers completed a two-game series with the Cincinnati Reds, the home club had taken yesterday's clash 6-2, routing young Harry Eisenstat.

Lloyd Moore, who had an unpleasant experience against the Brooks on the recent Eastern

Continued on Page 25.

Yanks Get 8 Runs Off Indians

BATTING ORDER.

CLEVELAND	YANKEES
Lary, ss	Crosetti, ss
Heath, rf	Rolfe, 3b
Averill, cf	DiMaggio, cf
Trosky, 1b	Gehrig, 1b
Solters, lf	Dickey, c
Hale, 2b	Selkirk, rf
Pytlak, c	Henrich, lf
Hughes, 3b	Lazzeri, 2b
Andrews, p	Chandler, p

Umpires — Quinn, Basil and Summers.

By Max Kase.

YANKEE STADIUM, May 24.—In a hitting mood again, the Yanks were hopeful of paying off an early season slight when they closed their two-game series with the Cleveland Indians here this afternoon.

Ivy Andrews was on the mound for the Indians, while Spurgeon Chandler, right-hander rookie, was making his third start for the Yanks.

Andrews blanked the world champions with only four hits in Cleveland on May 8, the first time the Yanks had been shut out since last July 12. Now that their bats have again found expression, 42 hits having been made in the last

Continued on Page 25.

3 Girls Chute

Flee Shelter Via Coal Route; All Caught

Three young girl inmates of the Children's Society Shelter, 105 Schermerhorn st., Brooklyn, who attempted to flee the institution via a coal chute, were found after a seven hours' search hiding behind a coal heap in the cellar.

Looking like miniatures in black face, the trio were hauled out! They offered the explanation that the "Sunday weather got the best of them."

According to officials of the Shelter, the girls are Margaret Madden, 15, of 51 Dean st.; Concetta De Monte, 13, of 32 Woodhull st., both Brooklyn, and Emily Swift, 15, of 128 Ft. Washington ave., The Bronx.

Rockefeller Rites Arranged for Wednesday

The mighty Rockefeller clan gathered at Pocantico Hills today in somber mourning for John D. Rockefeller, Sr., first of the world's billionaires.

In Ormond Beach, Fla., where he died yesterday at the age of 97, flags wavered at half staff as preparations were completed to ship his body north tonight.

Shortly before the body was to be placed aboard the train a brief religious ceremony was held. Only members of the household and a few intimate friends of the family attended. Two hymns, "Come Thou Fount of Every Blessing" and "No Night There," both favorites of Rockefeller, were sung by I. W. Ramsey.

BURIAL THURSDAY.

Funeral services for the modern Croesus, who amassed the greatest fortune on earth but could not realize his cheris[illegible] ambition to li[illegible] for a century, will be held on Wednesday at the 3,500-acre Po-

Continued on Page 2, Column 1.

U. S. Bonds Firm After Decision

Rise Slightly, Stock Market Irregular

A better market in Government bonds was the chief response of security markets today to the news that the Supreme Court had upheld the Social Security Law.

Federal issues had been firm from the opening, and moved up later for gains running to 6-32 of a point. Trading was not especially active. The rest of the bond market displayed a firm tone with high grade corporate issues pointing upward.

The stock market was little influenced, starting higher, sagging toward midday and then staging a slight recovery to present a highly irregular appearance.

(Details in Financial Pages.)

New Roosevelt Plan Puts Ban on Child Labor

By GEORGE DURNO,
International News Service Staff Correspondent.

WASHINGTON, May 24.—In one of the most important proposals of his White House incumbency, President Roosevelt today called upon this session of Congress to enact legislation giving the Government "some control over maximum hours, minimum wages, the evil of child labor and the exploitation of child labor."

A special message to Congress outlined his philosophy, which followed the essence of the outlawed NRA.

The President did not specify the maximum hours or minimum wages he desires. Congress, he said, should have little trouble in arriving at a basic formula.

Legislation will establish it on a flexible basis of a 35-to-40-hour week and a 40-cent-an-hour minimum wage.

The President said there should be little dispute with his proposal to rule out of interstate commerce the products of manufacturers who employ child labor, who deny workers the right of self-organization and collective bargaining and who fail to meet minimum working standards.

In connection with the right of

Continued on Page 11, Column 1.

Gladys Defies State's Ax-Killing Accusation

Gladys MacKnight turned tigress today in a stunned Jersey City courtroom as she snarled her denial that she brutally hacked her mother to death with a hatchet in her Bayonne home last July 31.

Steeled against the cross-examination o Prosecutor Daniel T. O'Regan, the 17-year-old high school graduate, seemed ready to spring at him from the witness box as he opened a scathing attack on her story that her choir boy lover, Donald Wightman, and not she wielded the axe that slew her mother.

Gladys leaned forward in her chair, her shoulders hunched, her eyes sparkling and her teeth flashing, as she met the prosecutor's questions with snarled answers.

ANGERED BY QUERIES.

Anger flared at the first question of O'Regan.

At times she was freezingly polite in her replies . . . and again she fairly shouted her denials.

A shocked jury heard the "tiger

Continued on Page 10, Column 4.

TODAY'S JOURNAL

[illegible]

International News Service and Universal Service, Telegraph, Cable and Radio Dispatches.

Entered as Second-Class Matter, Post Office, New York, N. Y.

3d Son Born to Lindys in England

CLEVELAND, May 24 (By International News Service). — Birth of a third son to Col. and Mrs. Charles A. Lindbergh in England 12 days ago was disclosed here today by relatives of Mrs. Lindbergh, the former Anne Morrow.

The information was contained in a letter received Saturday by Mrs. Charles Long Cutter, grandmother of Mrs. Lindbergh.

The letter was written by Mrs. Dwight Morrow, a daughter of Mrs. Cutter and mother of Mrs. Lindbergh.

The baby was born on May 12, according to Miss Annie Cutter, a sister of Mrs. Morrow. Reached at Cleveland Public Library, where she is head of the schools department, Miss Cutter said:

"We received a letter Saturday giving us the news of the birth of a baby boy, on Coronation Day, to Mrs. Lindbergh.

"When the letter was written, both mother and child were very well. I believe that at that time the baby had not as yet been named."

Mrs. Cutter, who is approaching her 92nd birthday, was "very, very happy" at the news, Miss Cutter said.

Interviewers were not permitted to talk with Mrs. Cutter. They

Continued on Page 9, Column 1.

Honk, Honk!

Who drove the first automobile on Riverside Drive? It must have been a Neotrist . . . a person who Stays Young . . . because the Neotrist descendants of that pioneer motorist of the nineties are still thronging the old Drive, merrily buying $63,000,000 worth of automobiles every year!

the Neotrist

A RADICALLY DIFFERENT FRONT PAGE

In 1934 the Graduate School of Journalism developed a front-page layout in which the masthead was set at left and a picture displayed in the upper right corner. This principle was recently adopted in somewhat different form by The New York Journal.